Food and Snacks Coloring book

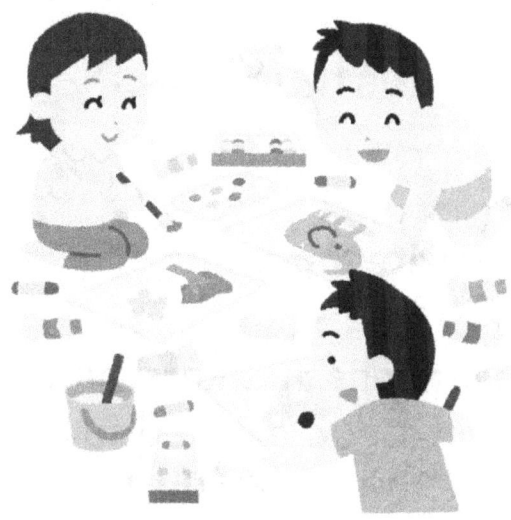

This book belongs to:

FOOD AND SNACKS
CHILDREN'S WORKSHEET

Welcome to the food and snack coloring worksheets! Activate your Unleash your creativity and add bright colors to these delicious foods and snacks.
Follow these instructions to design your painting experience

INSTRUCTIONS

1. Choose Food:
Choose your favorite foods and snacks from the list.

2. Color:
Use crayons, markers, or paint Pencils for coloring food. Get creative and use whatever you want Color you like!

3. Stay within the lines:
Try to paint within the lines of each color Food items. It's okay to go out for a little walk!

4. Add details:
Do you want to add extra toppings? decorate? do it! Make your food look extra delicious.

5. Show off:
Share your Once coloring is complete, paint a masterpiece with friends and family. You will love watching it Your delicious meal!

6. Have fun:
The most important thing is to have fun! color is everything Let your imagination run wild. Have fun These foods come to life with color!

LET'S START CREATING SOMETHING COLORFUL FOOD MAGIC!

GRAPES

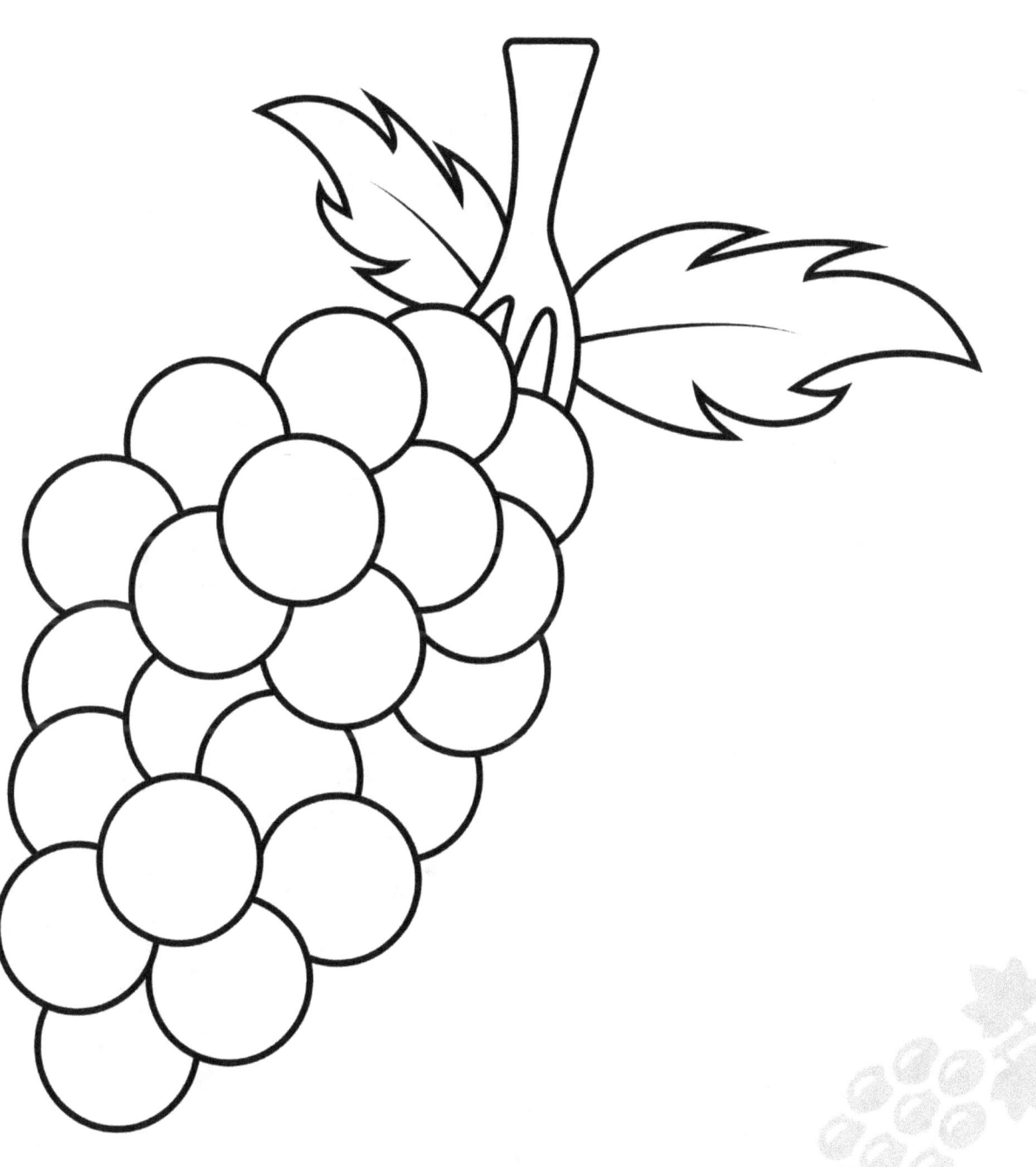

PEAR

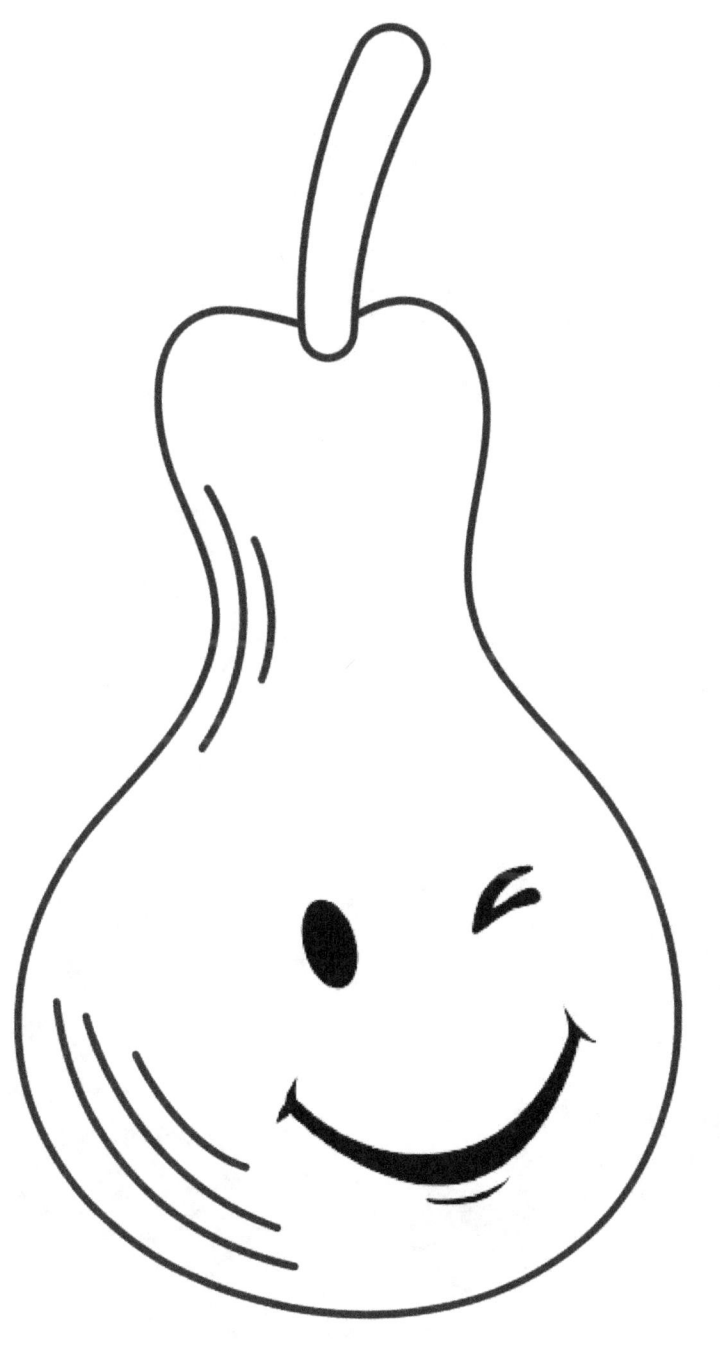

APPLE

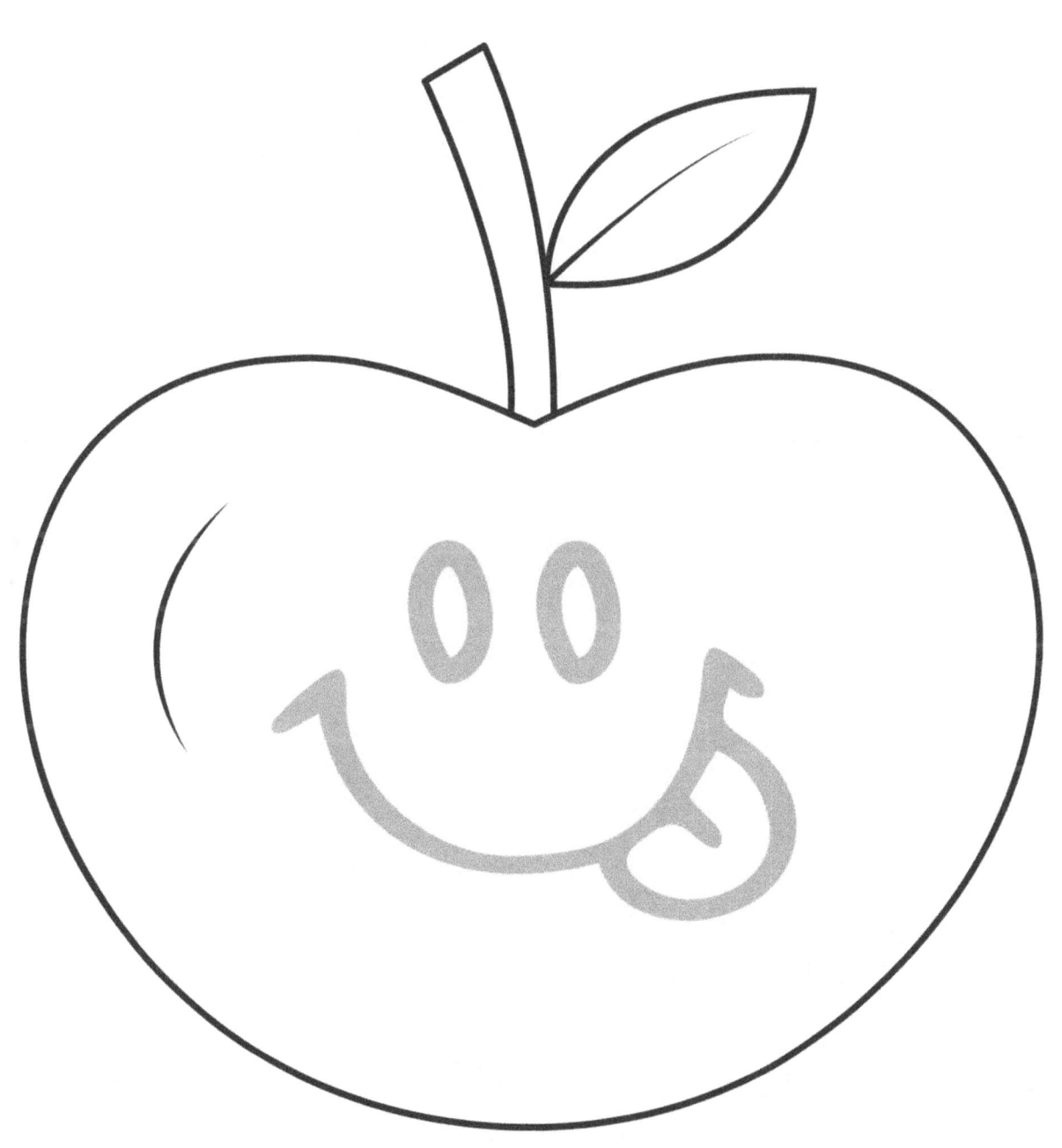

PEPPER

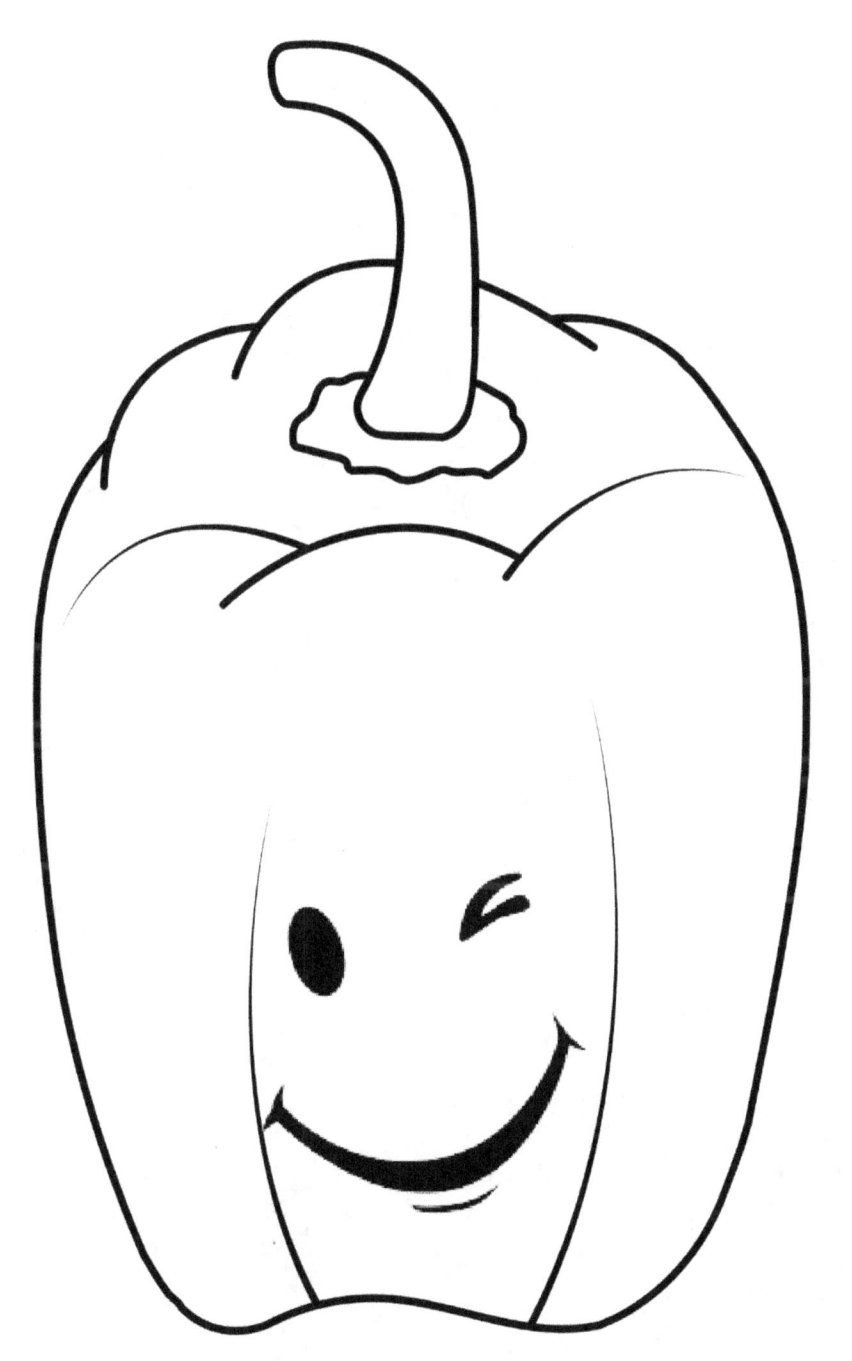

MANGO

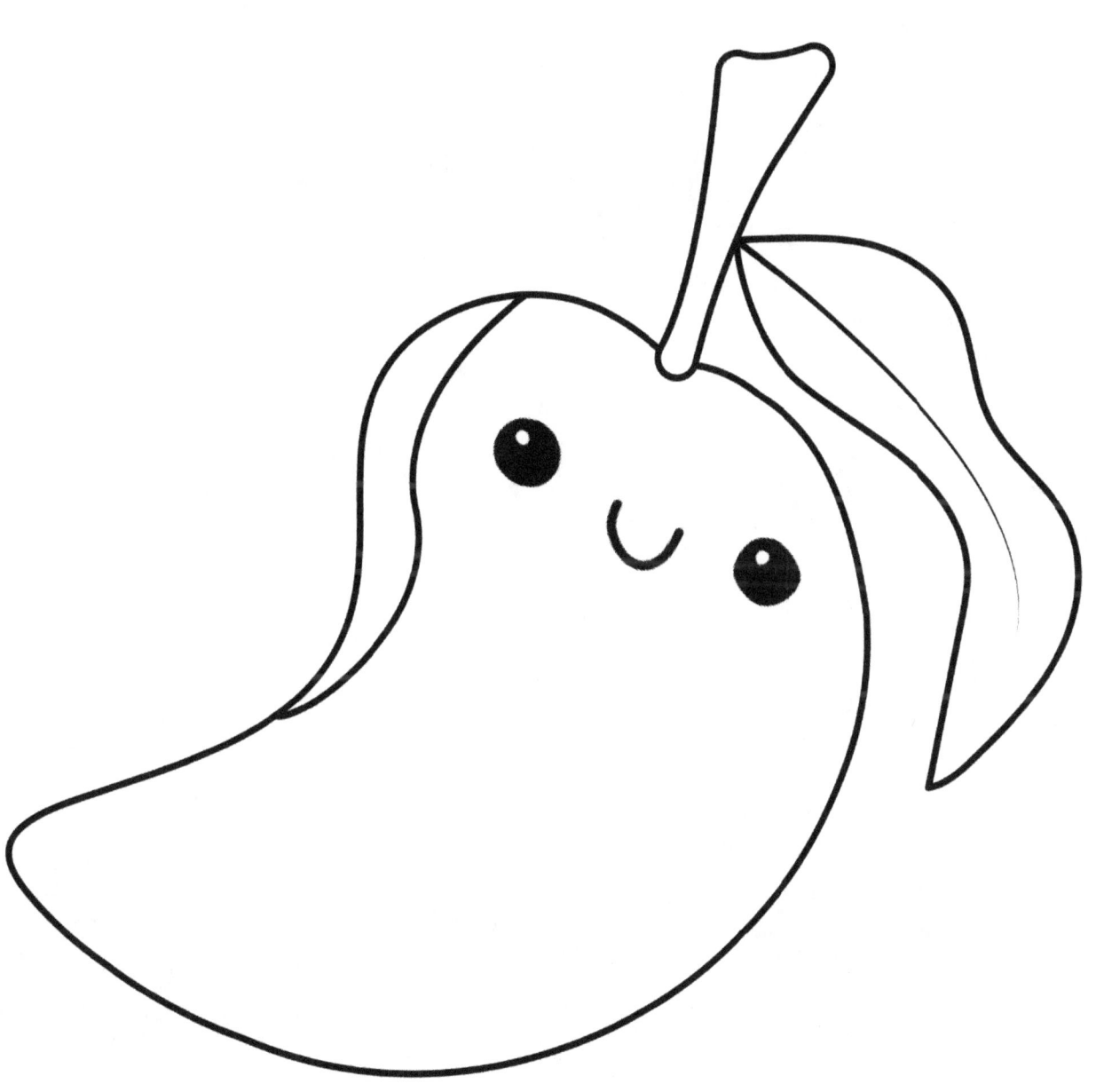

ตอนที่๓

TOMATO

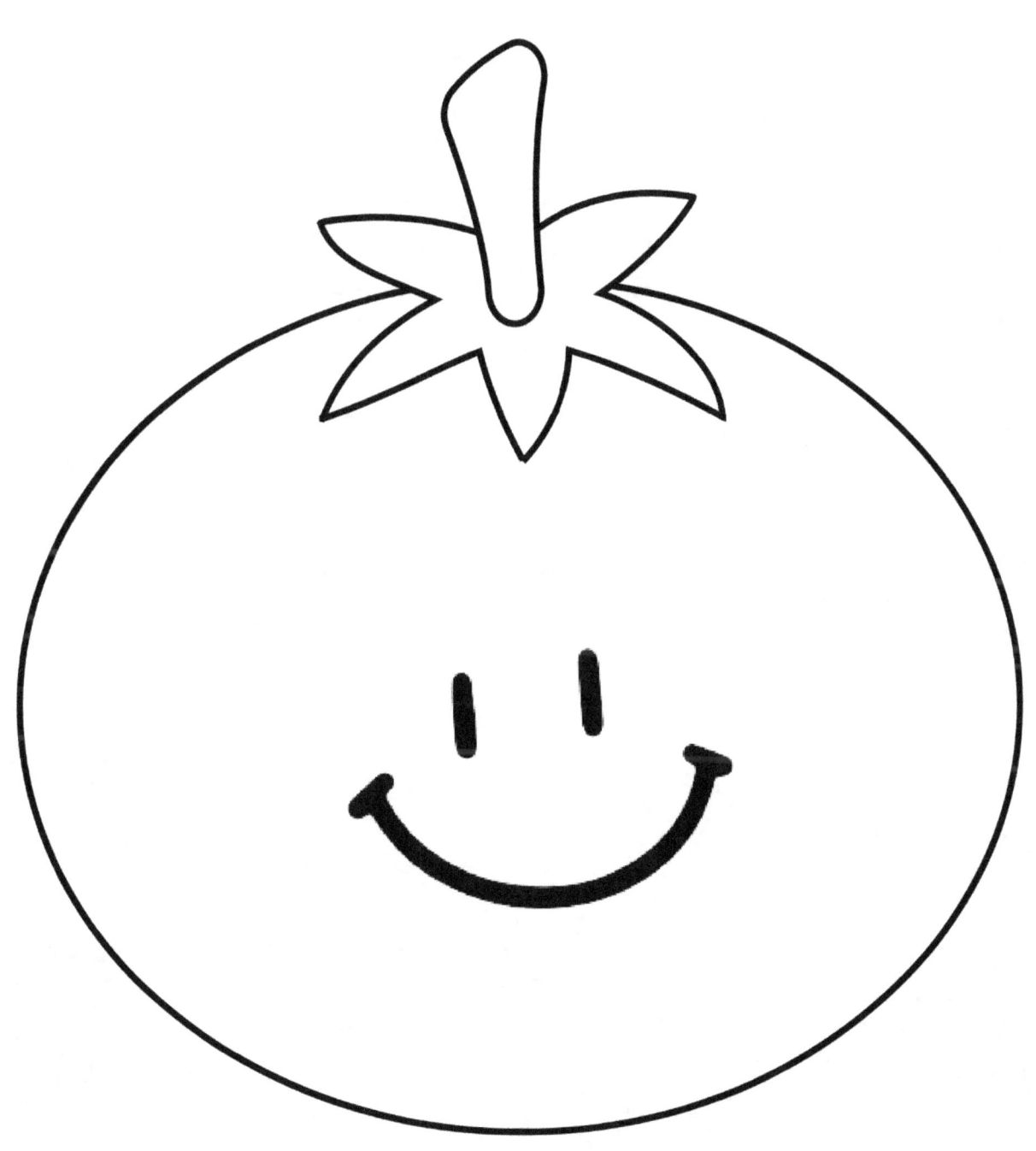

PUMPKIN

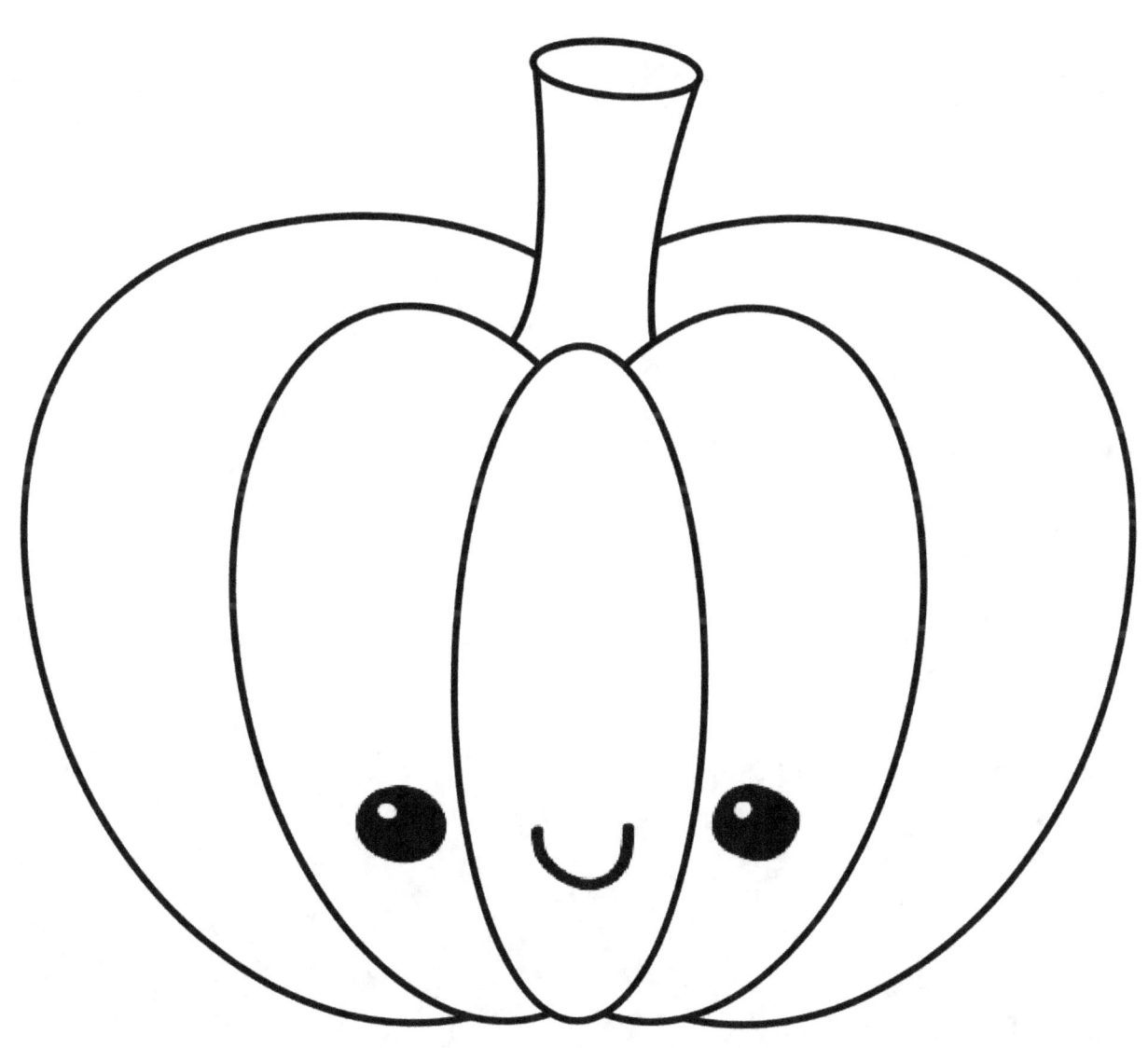

ORANGE

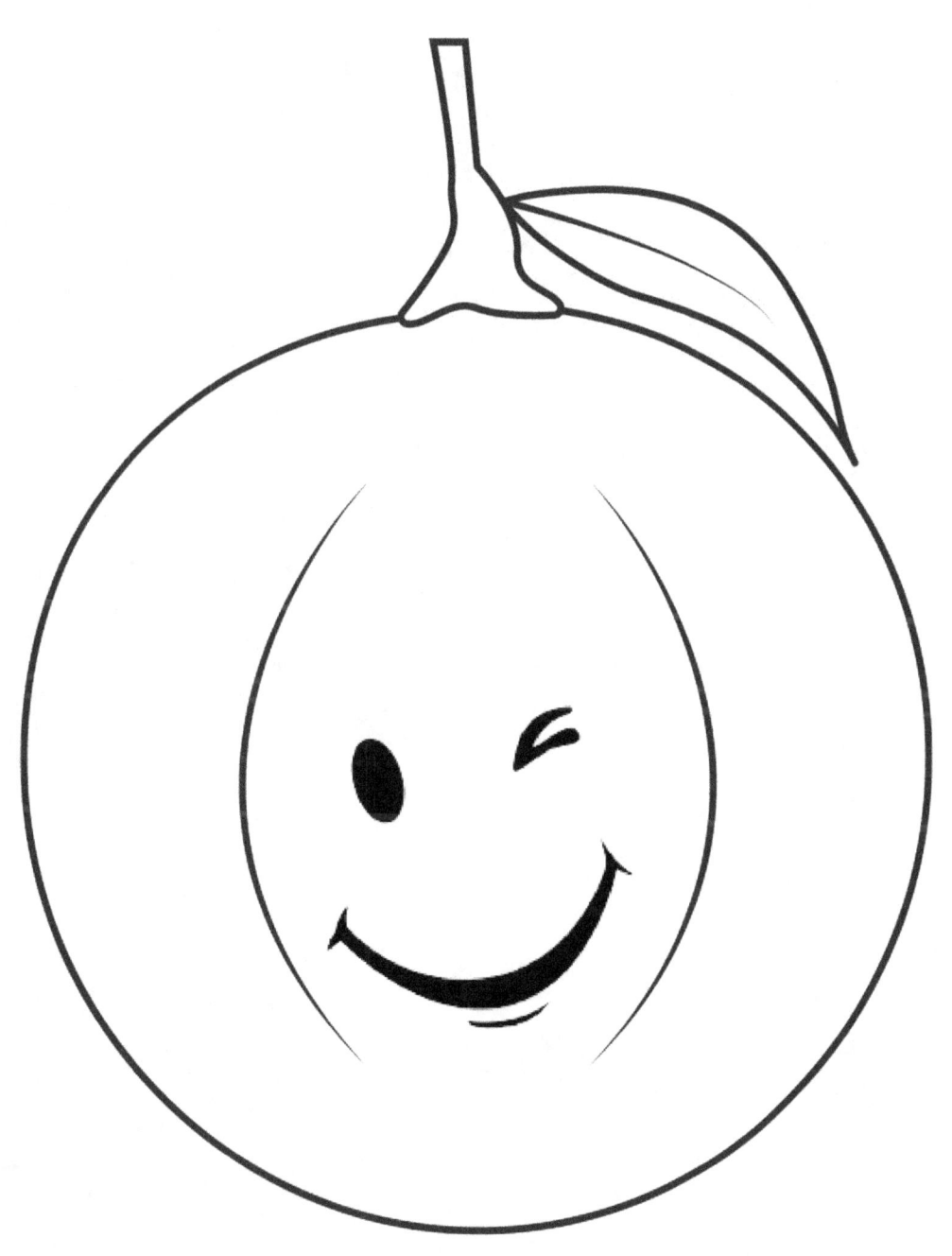

CARROT

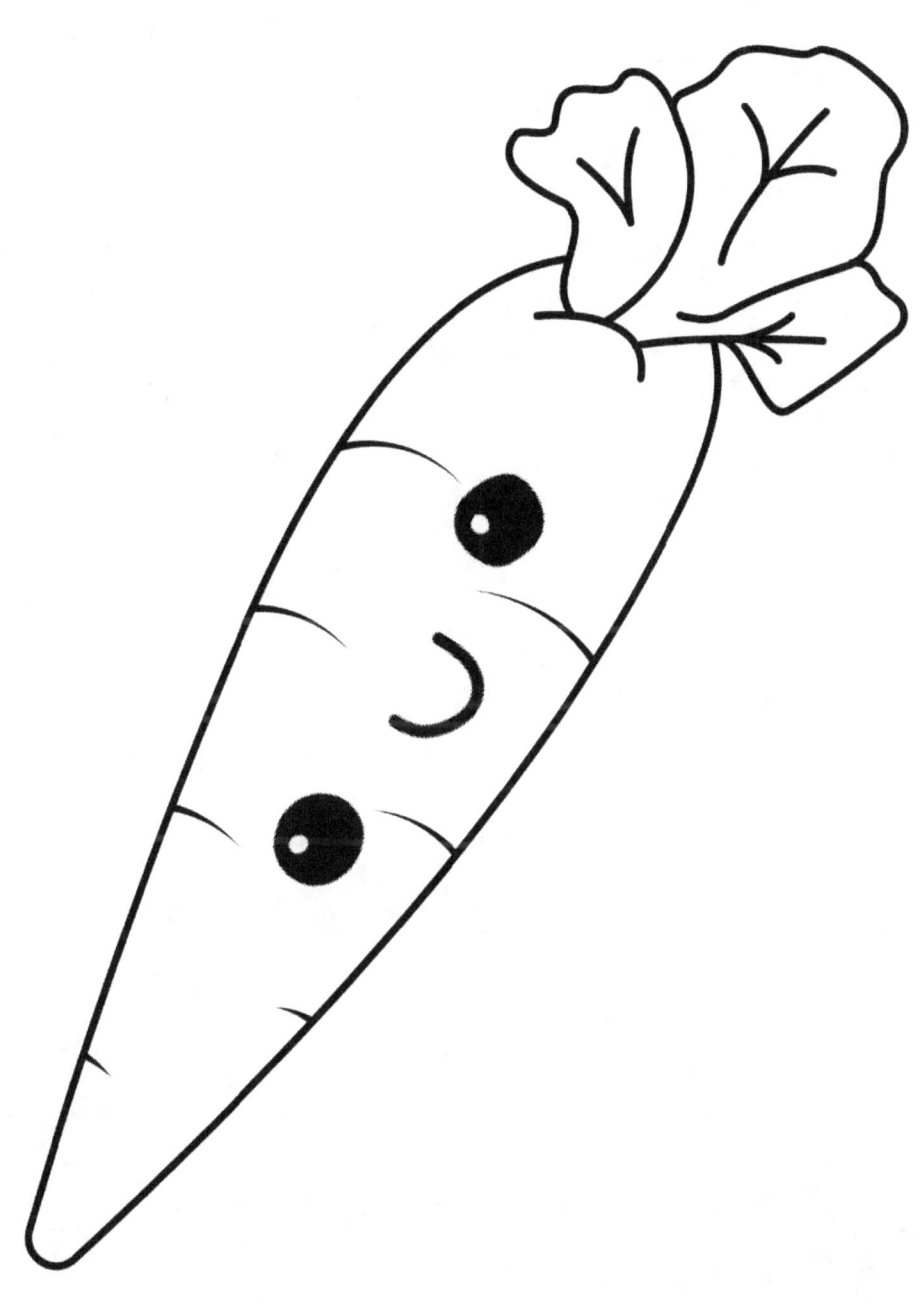

CARROT

BLUEBERRY

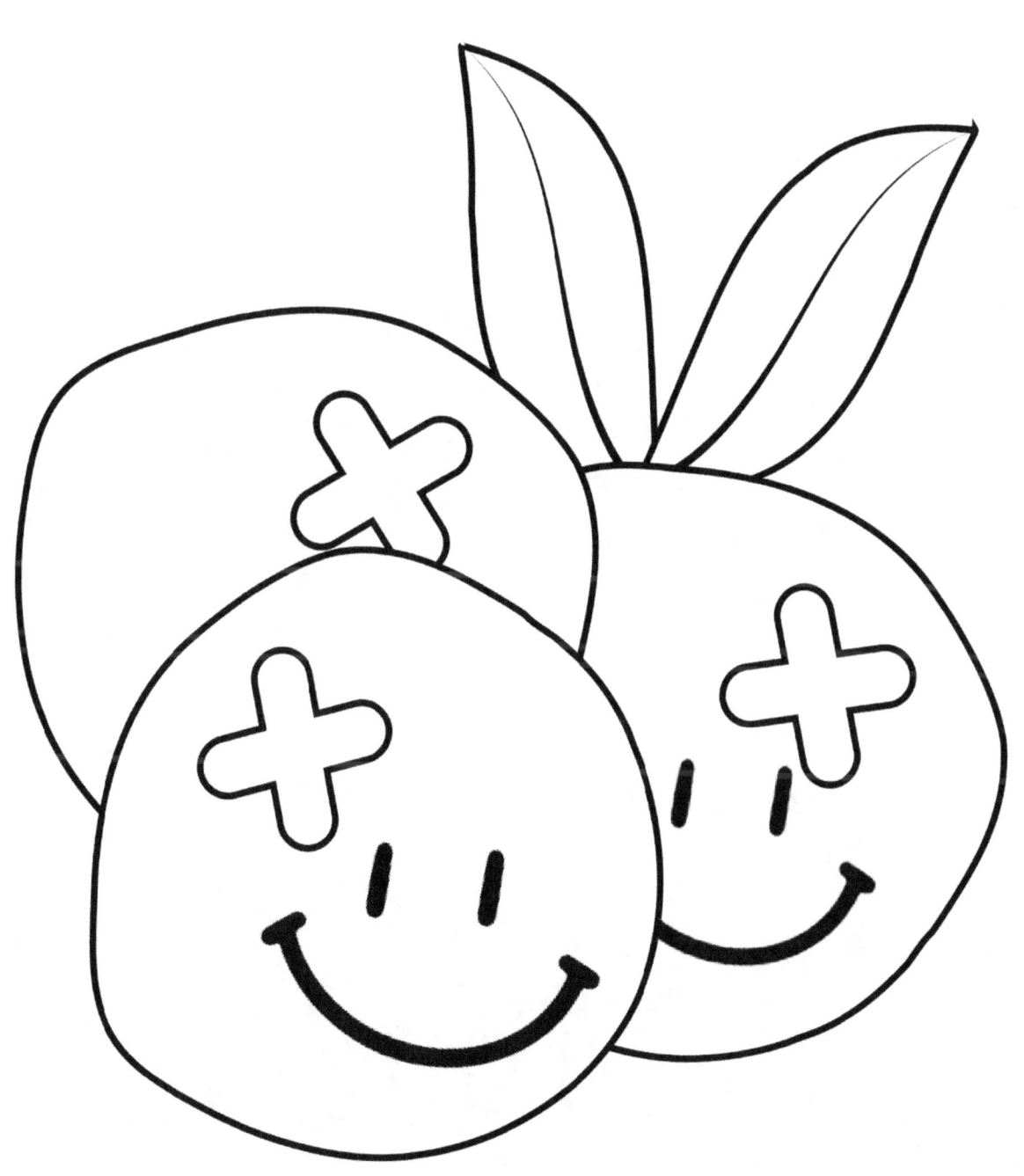

BANANA

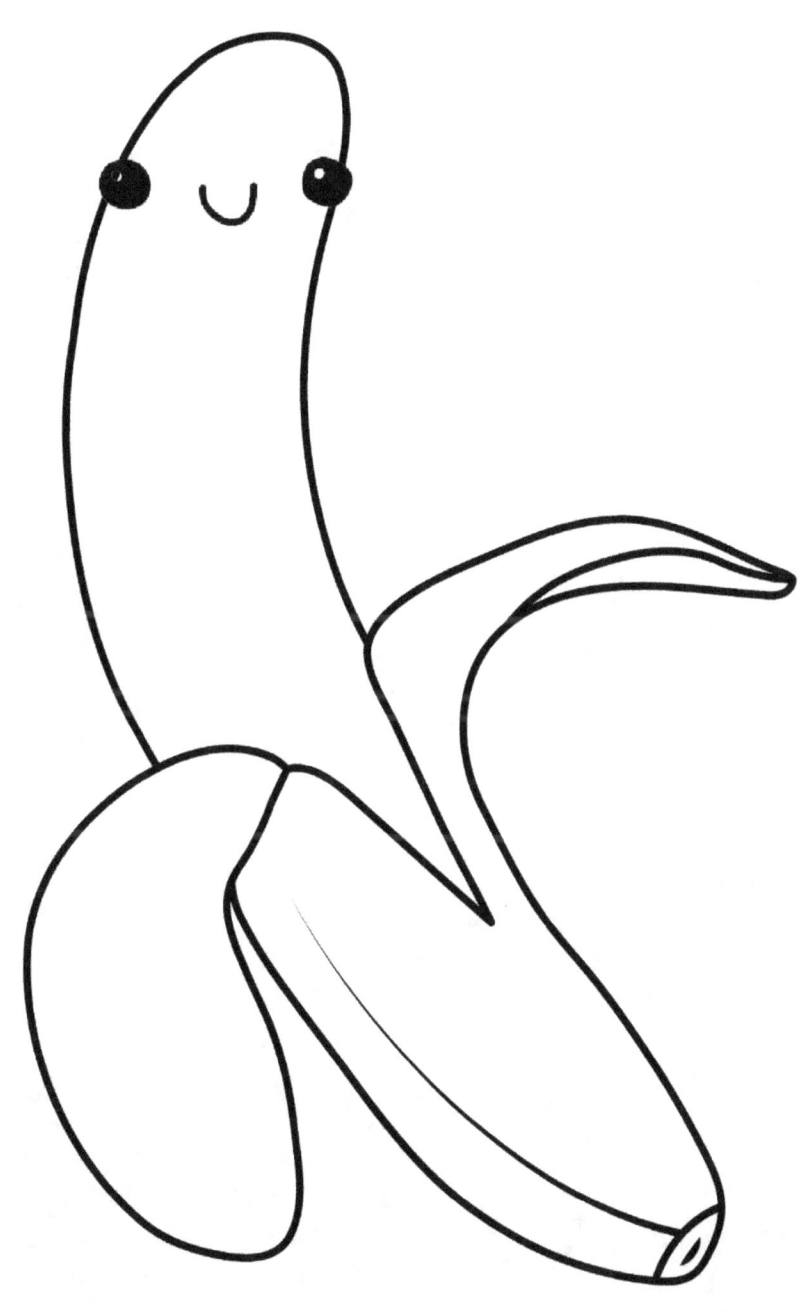

BANANA

BROCCOLI

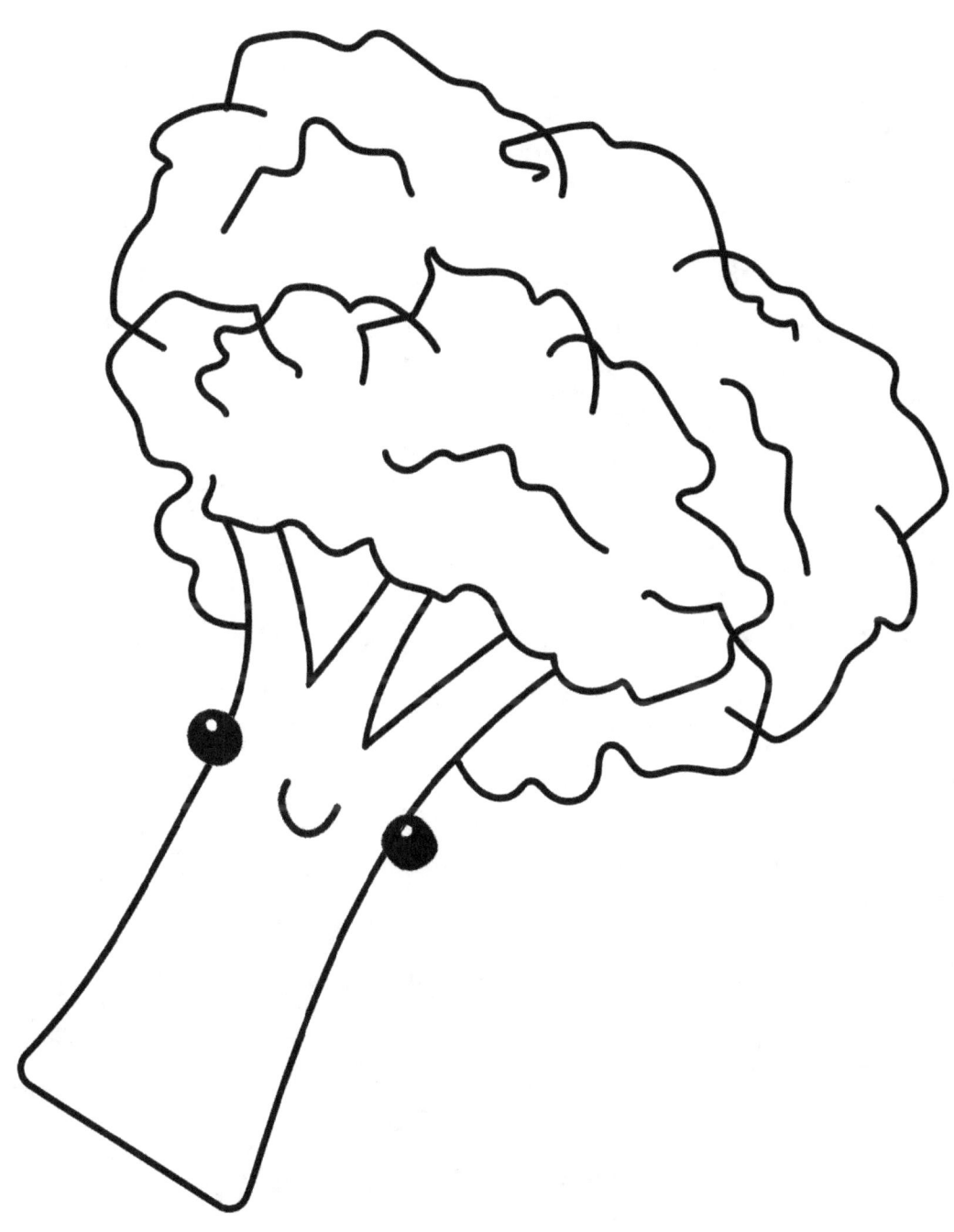

STRAWBERRY

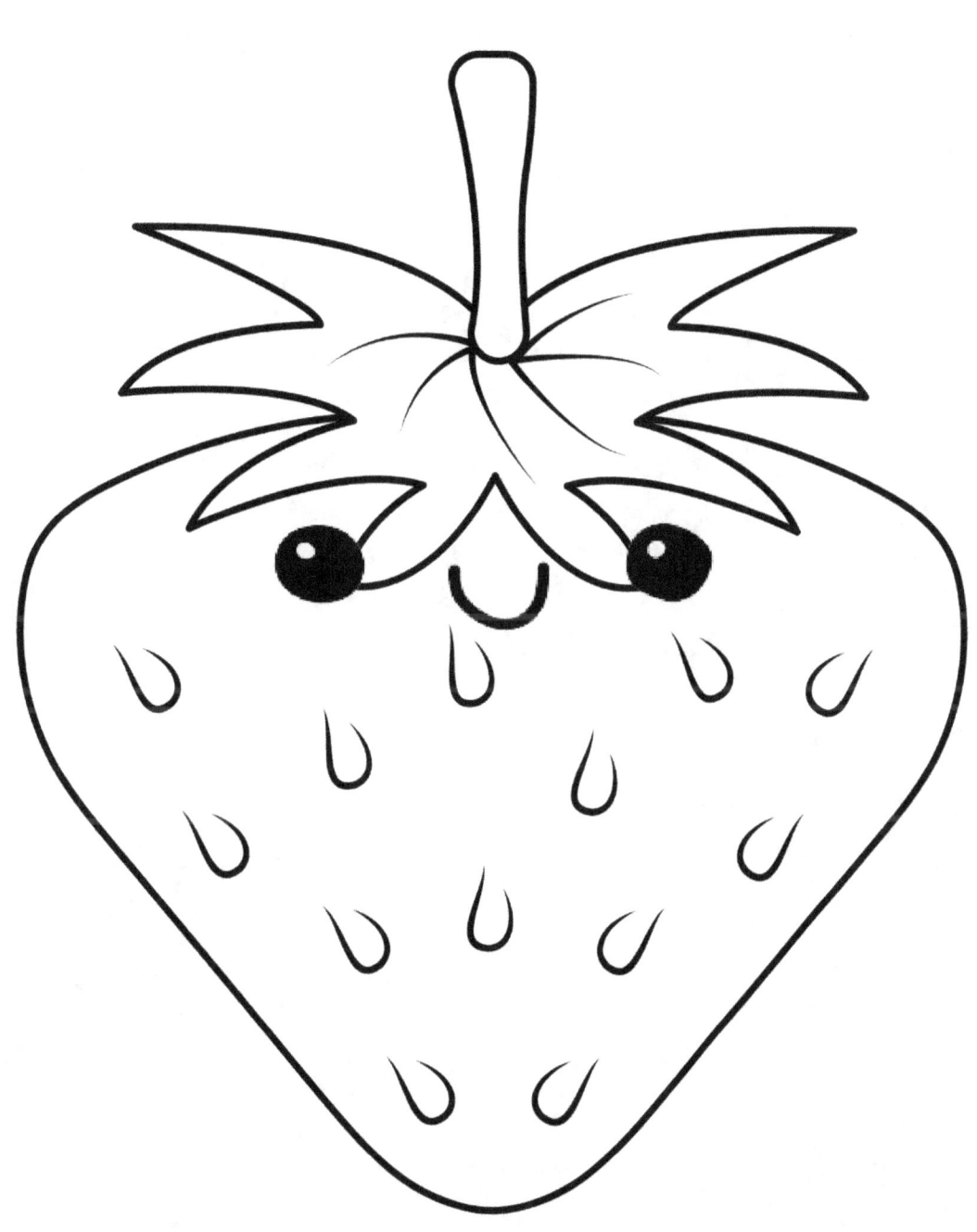

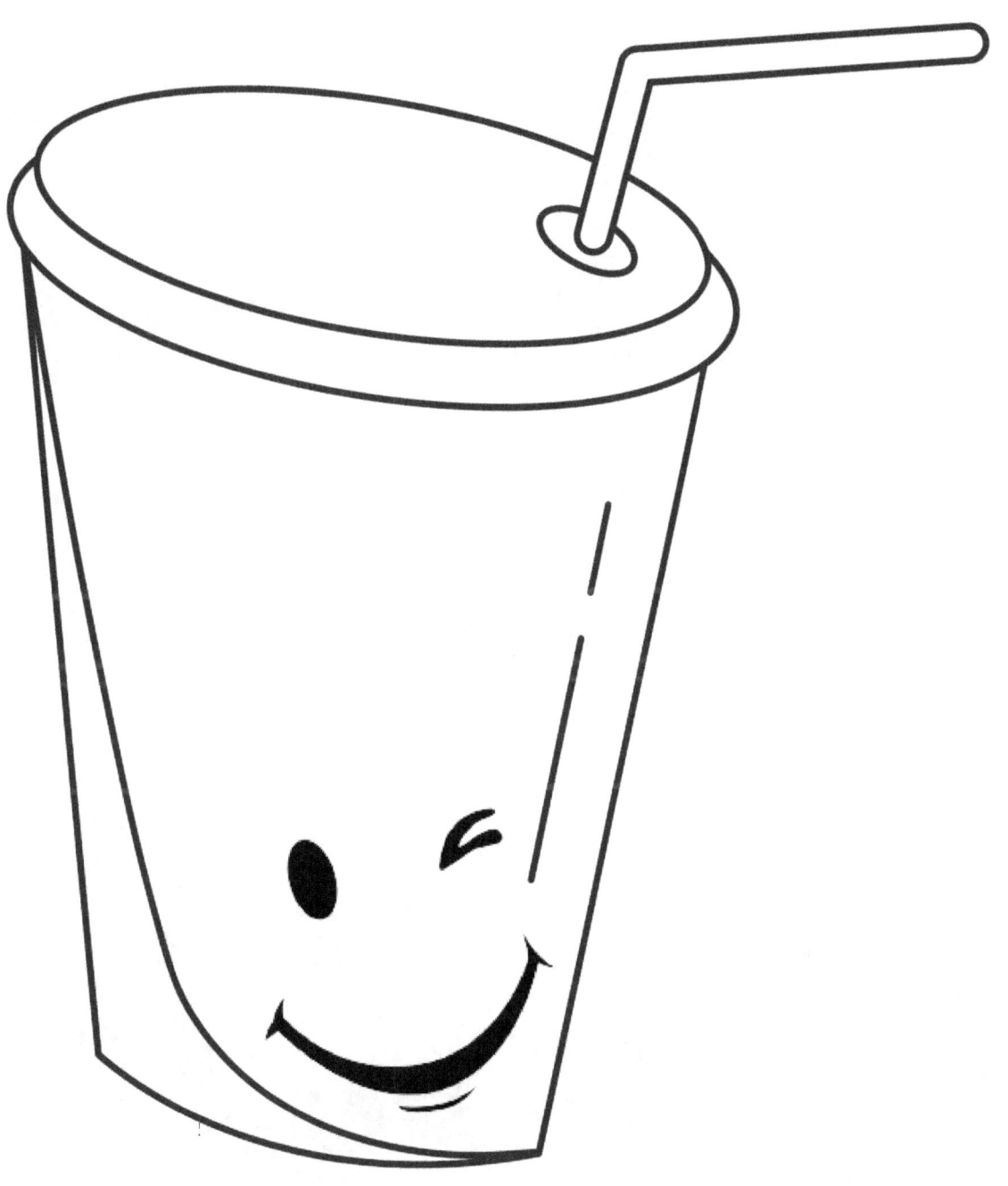

MEAT

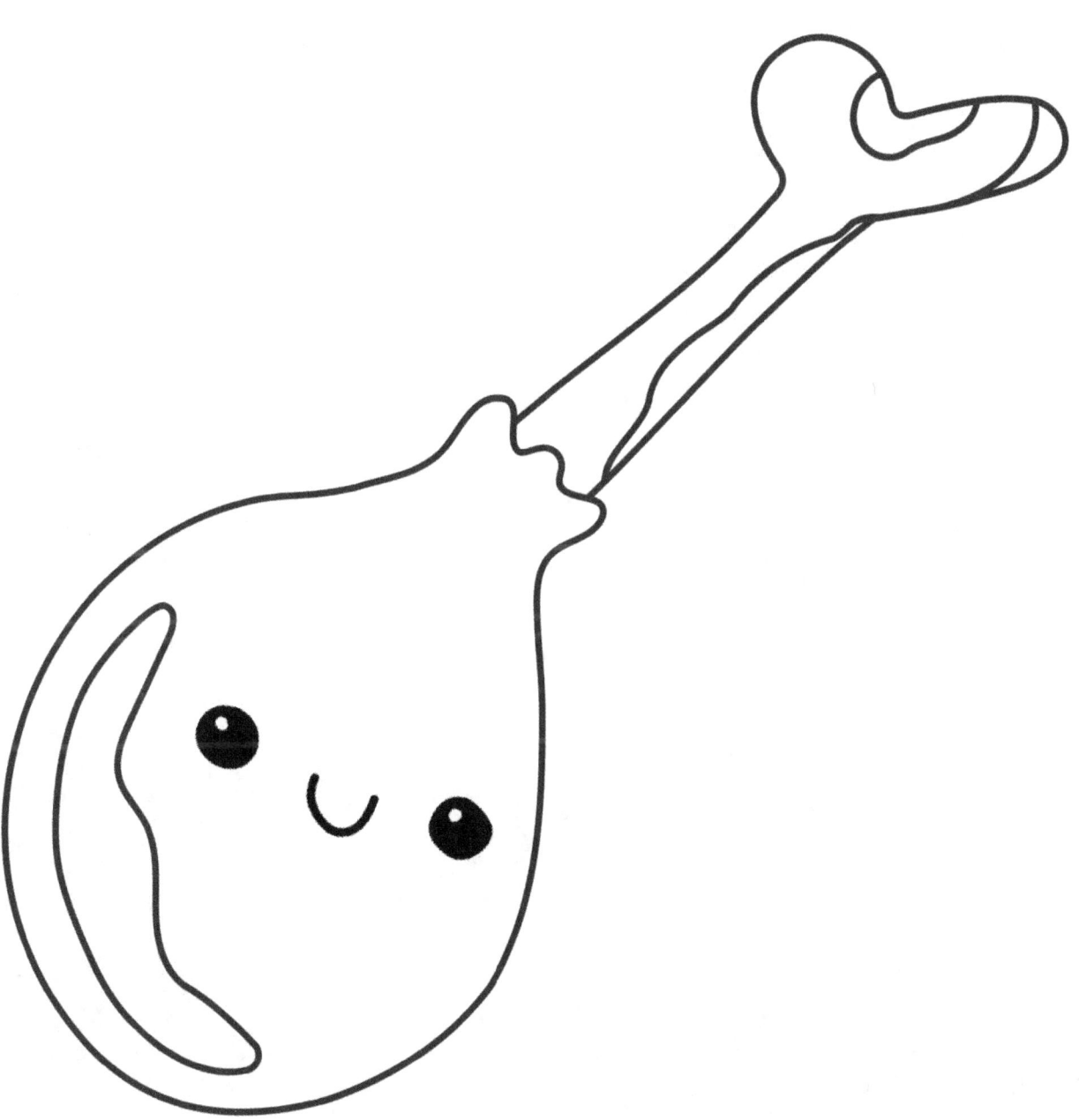

PEANUT

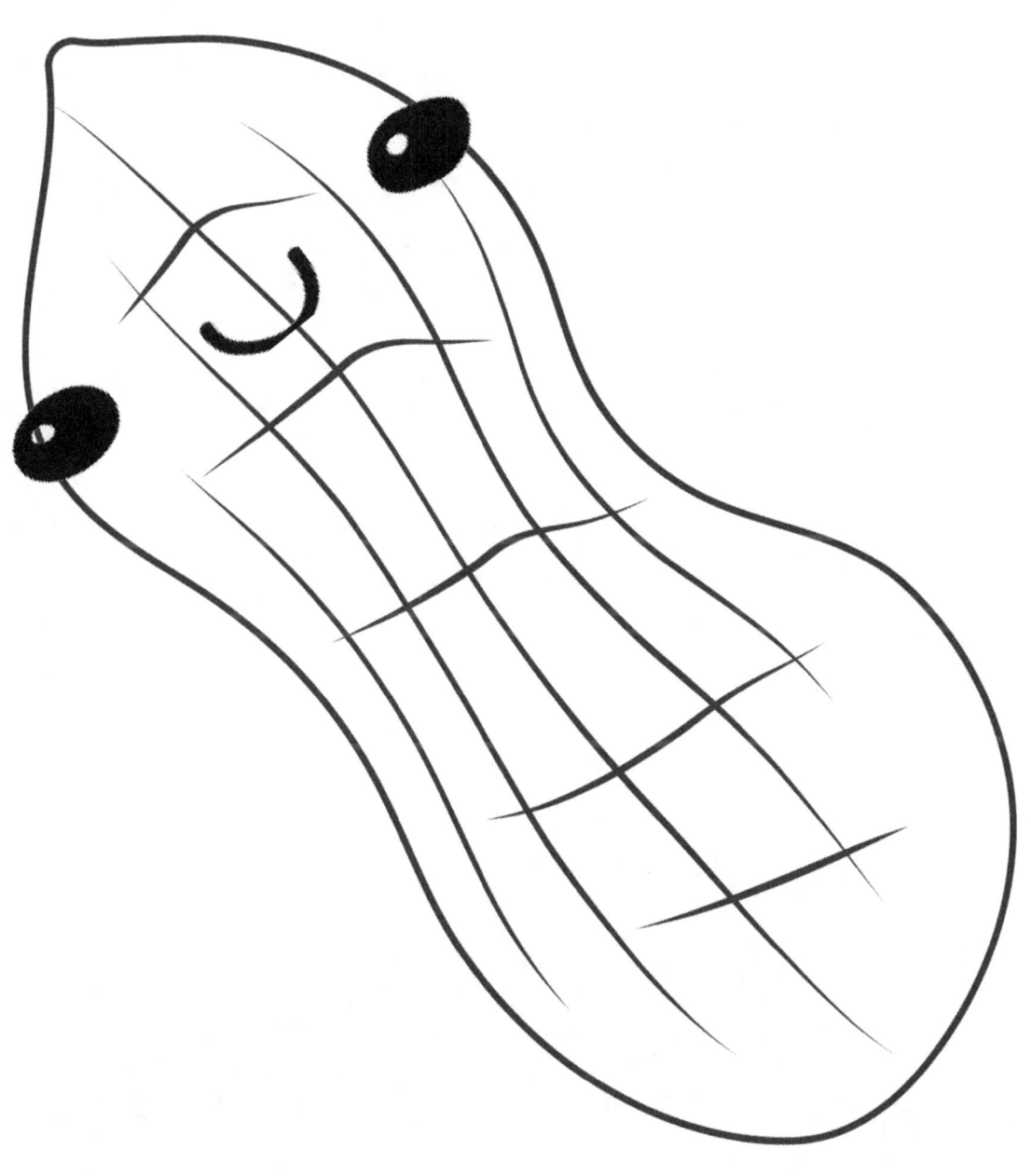

CHOCOLATE

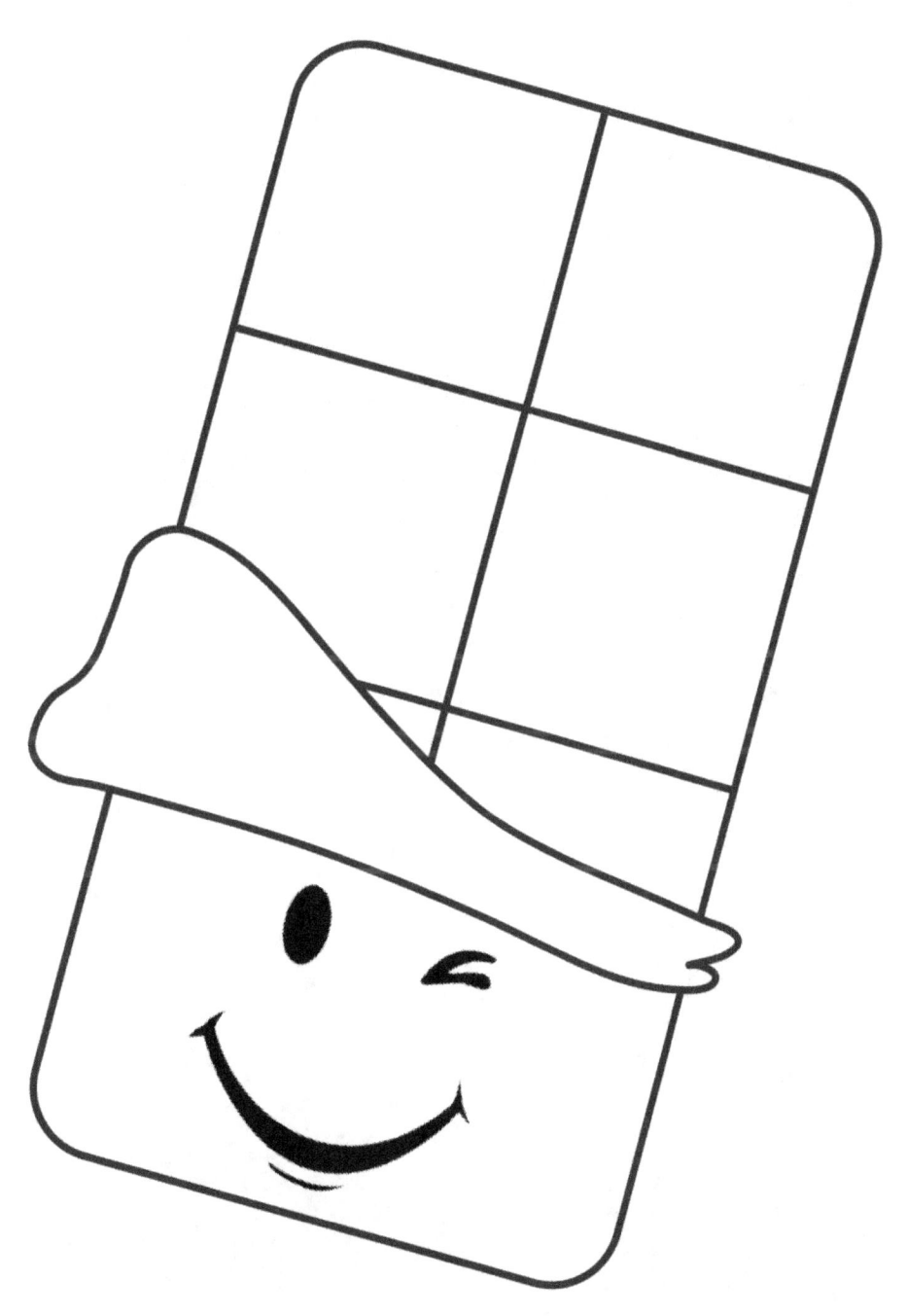

GRANOLA BAR

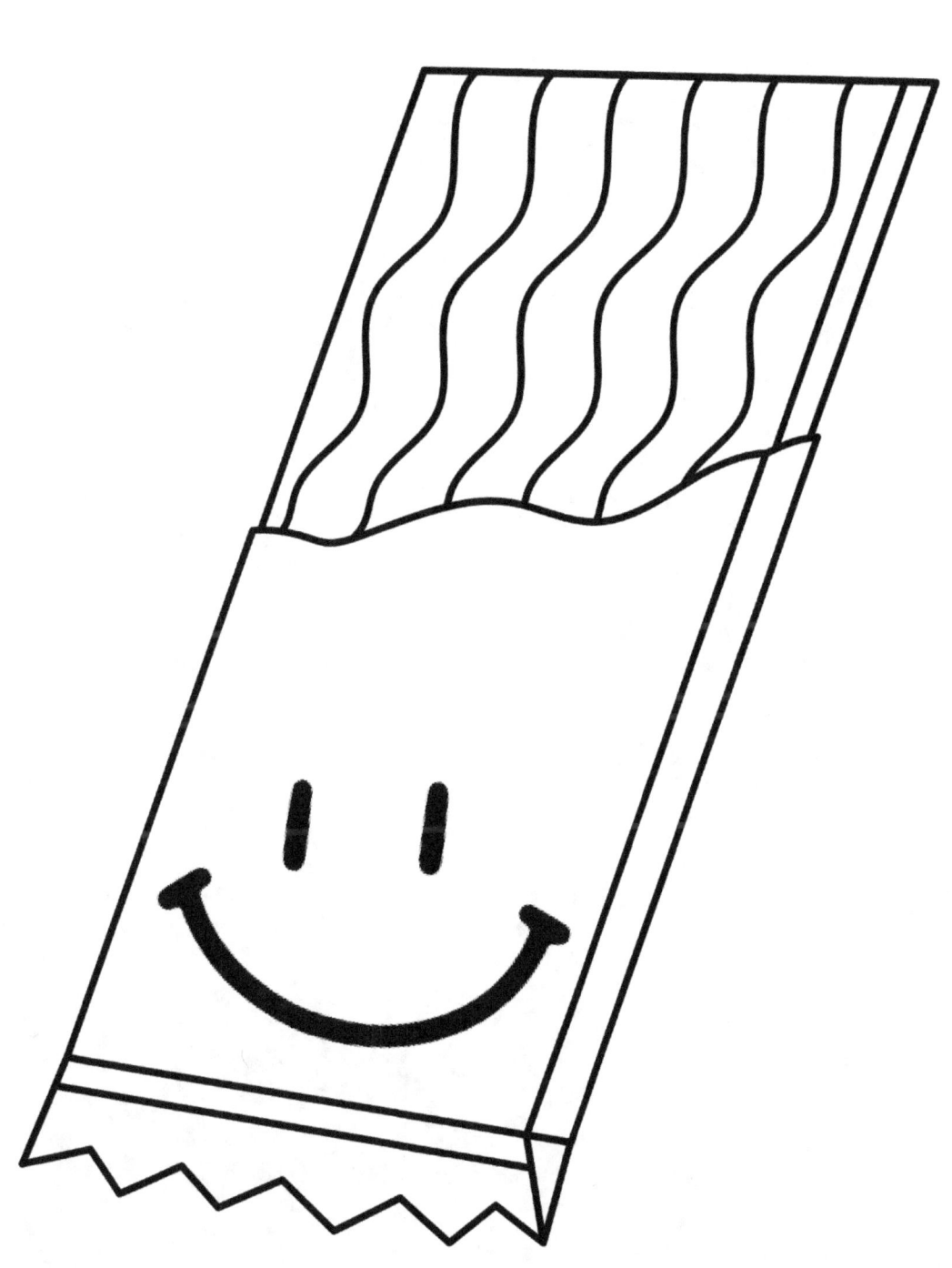

COFFEE CUP

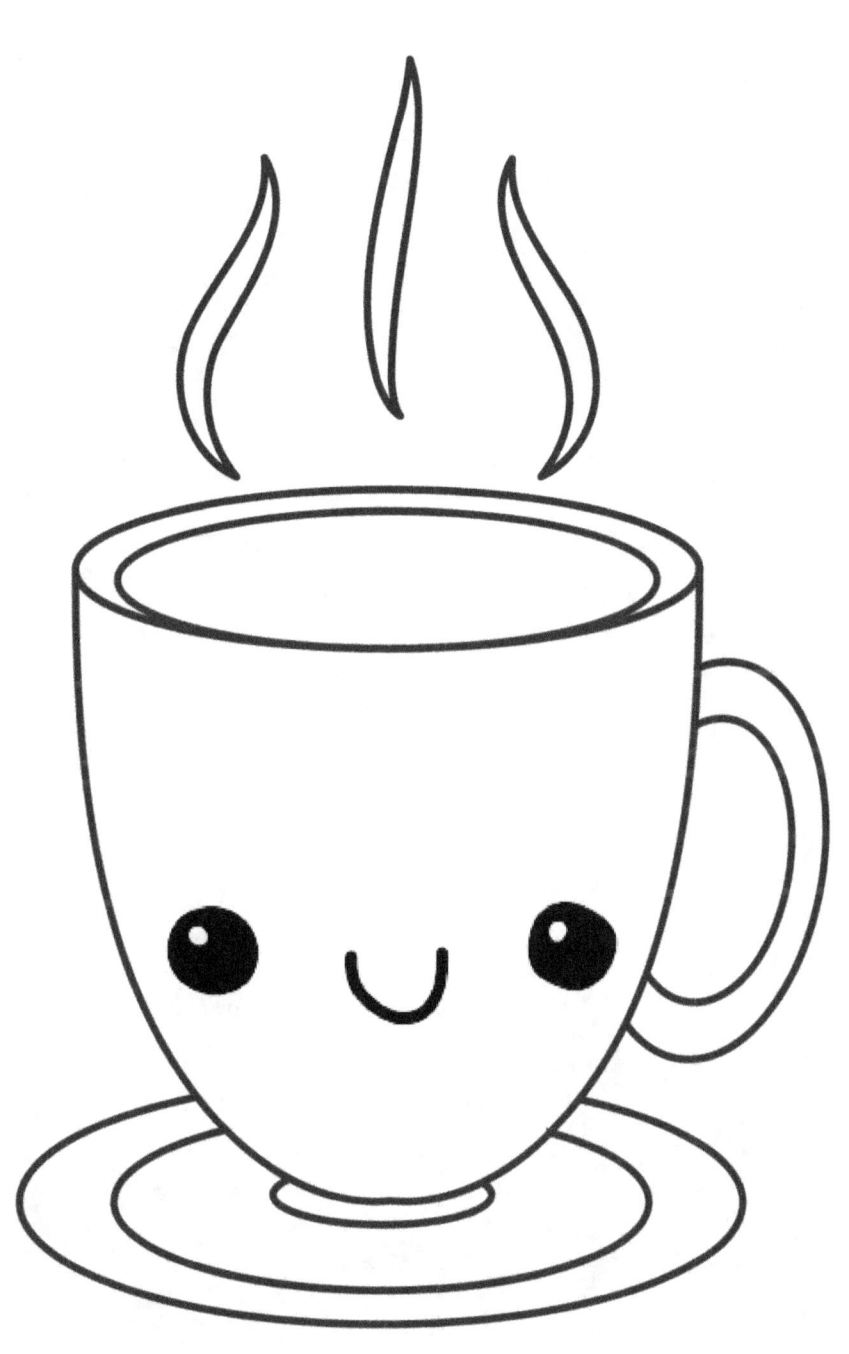

CUPCAKE

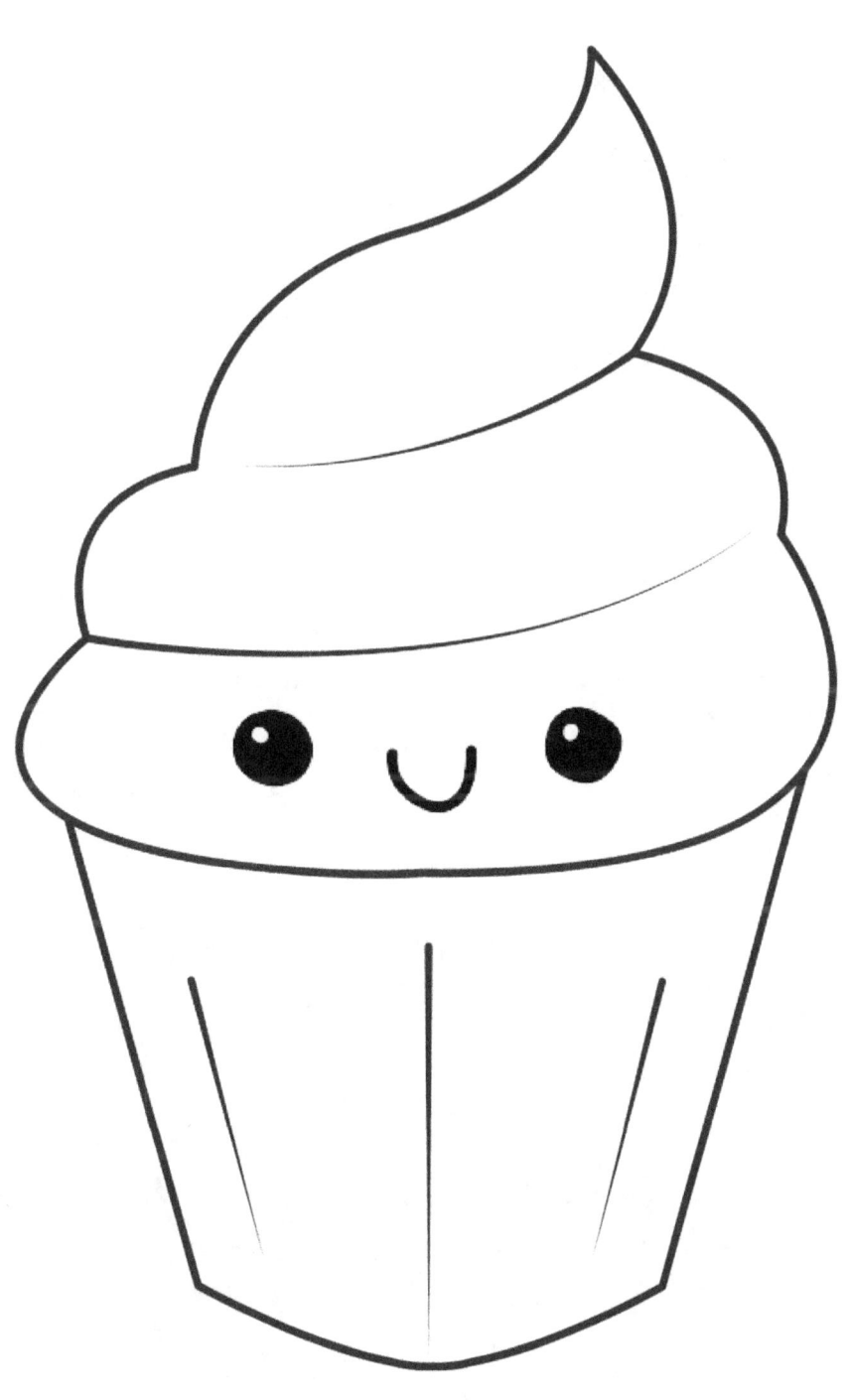

BREAD

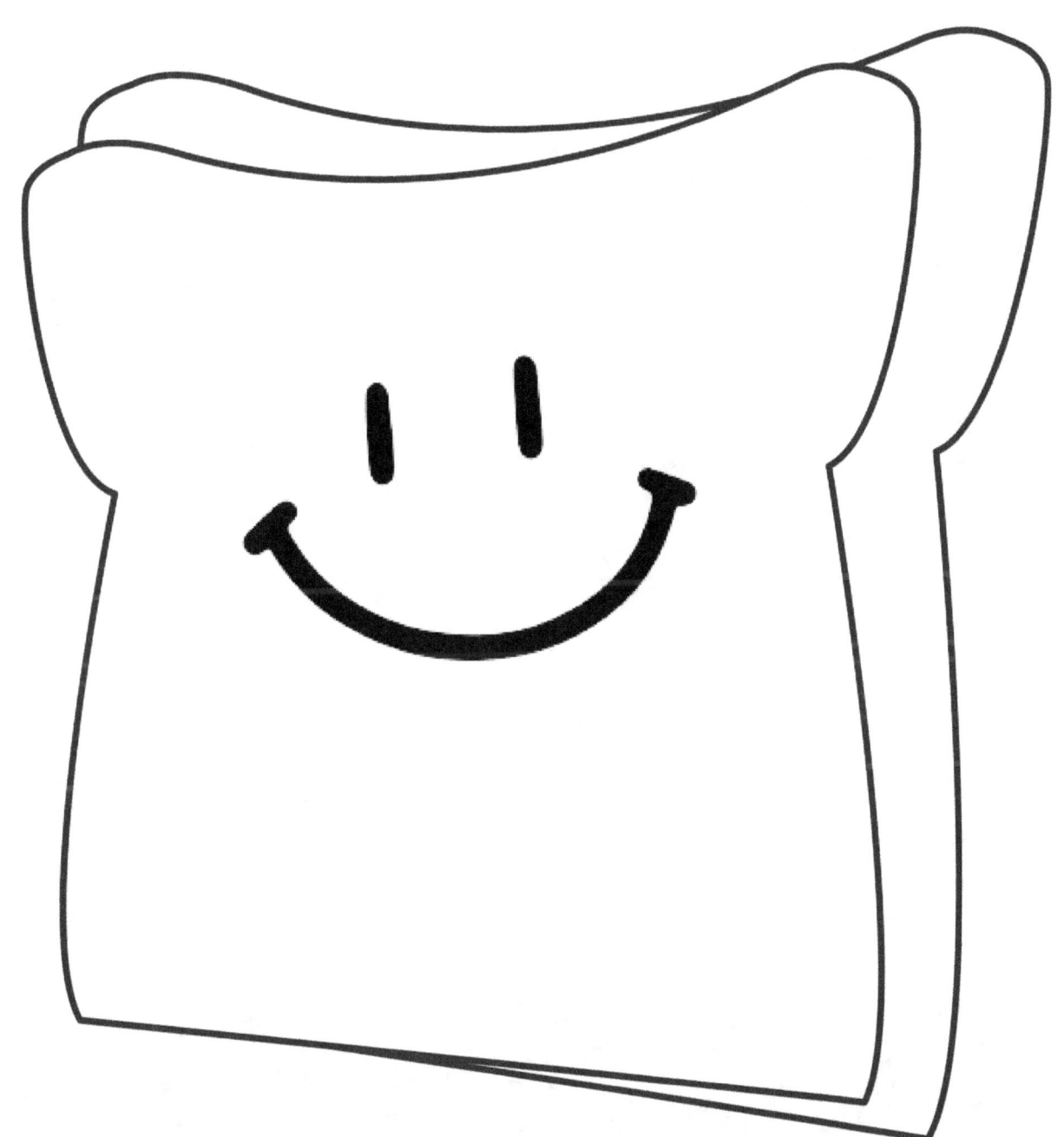

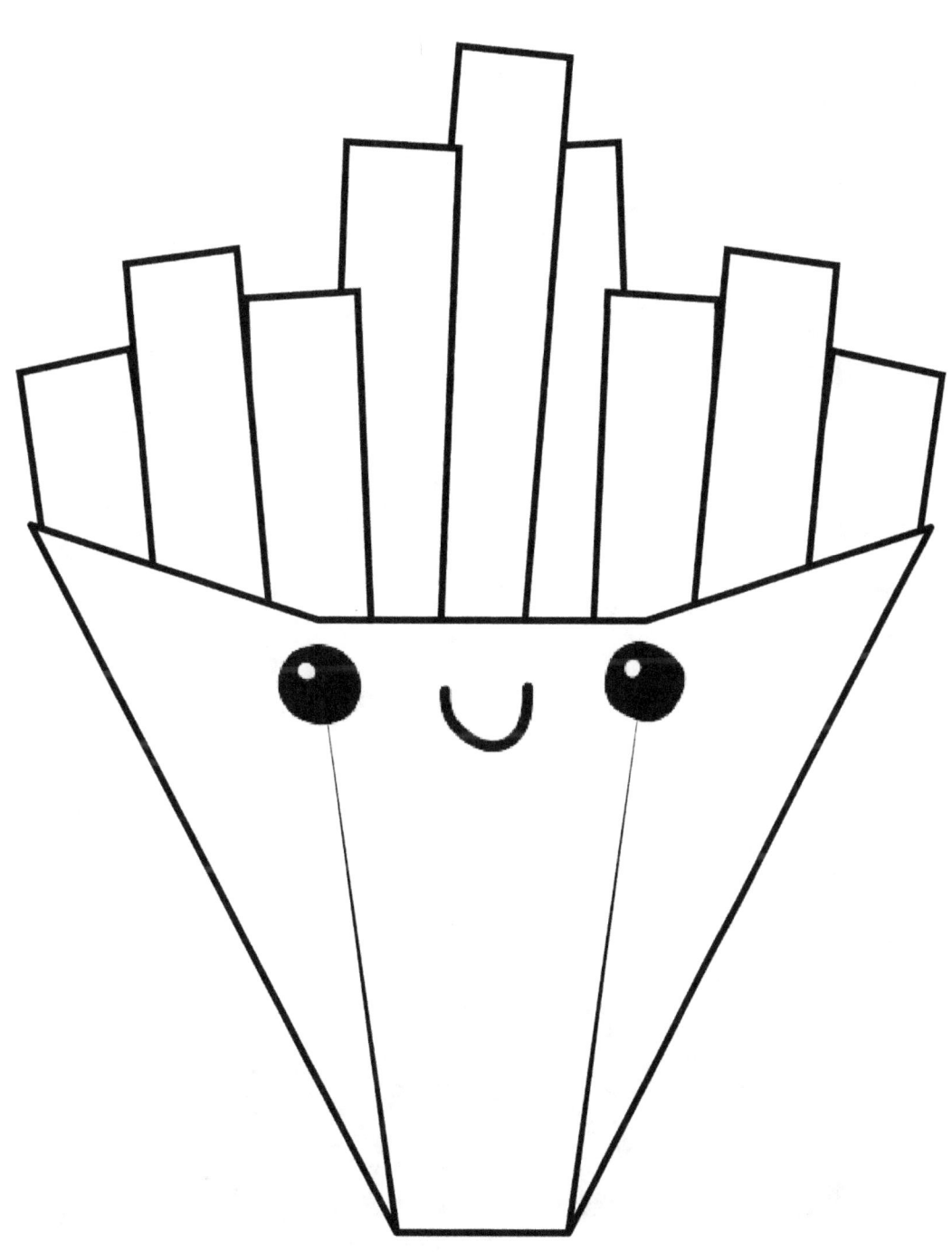

WATERMELON

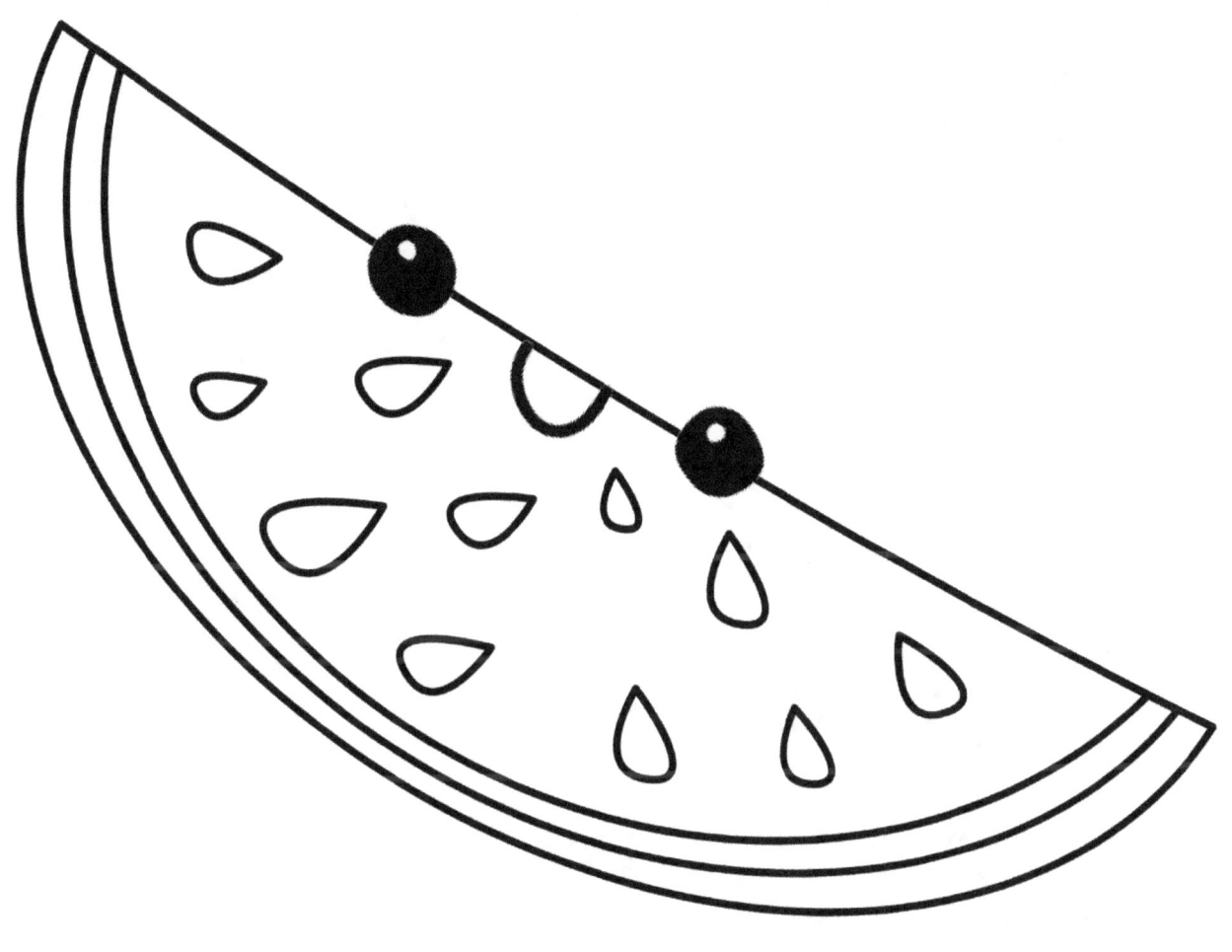

CORN

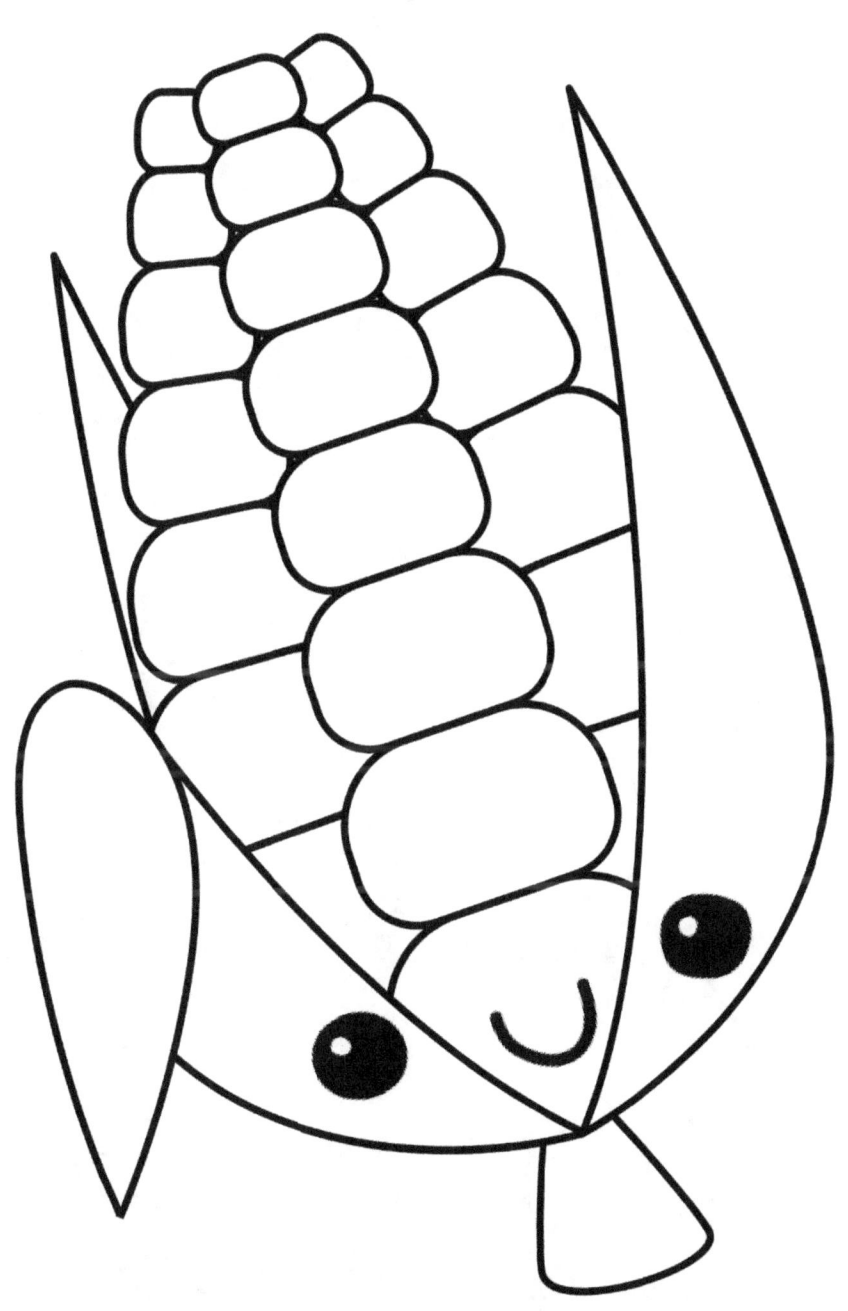

TEA POT

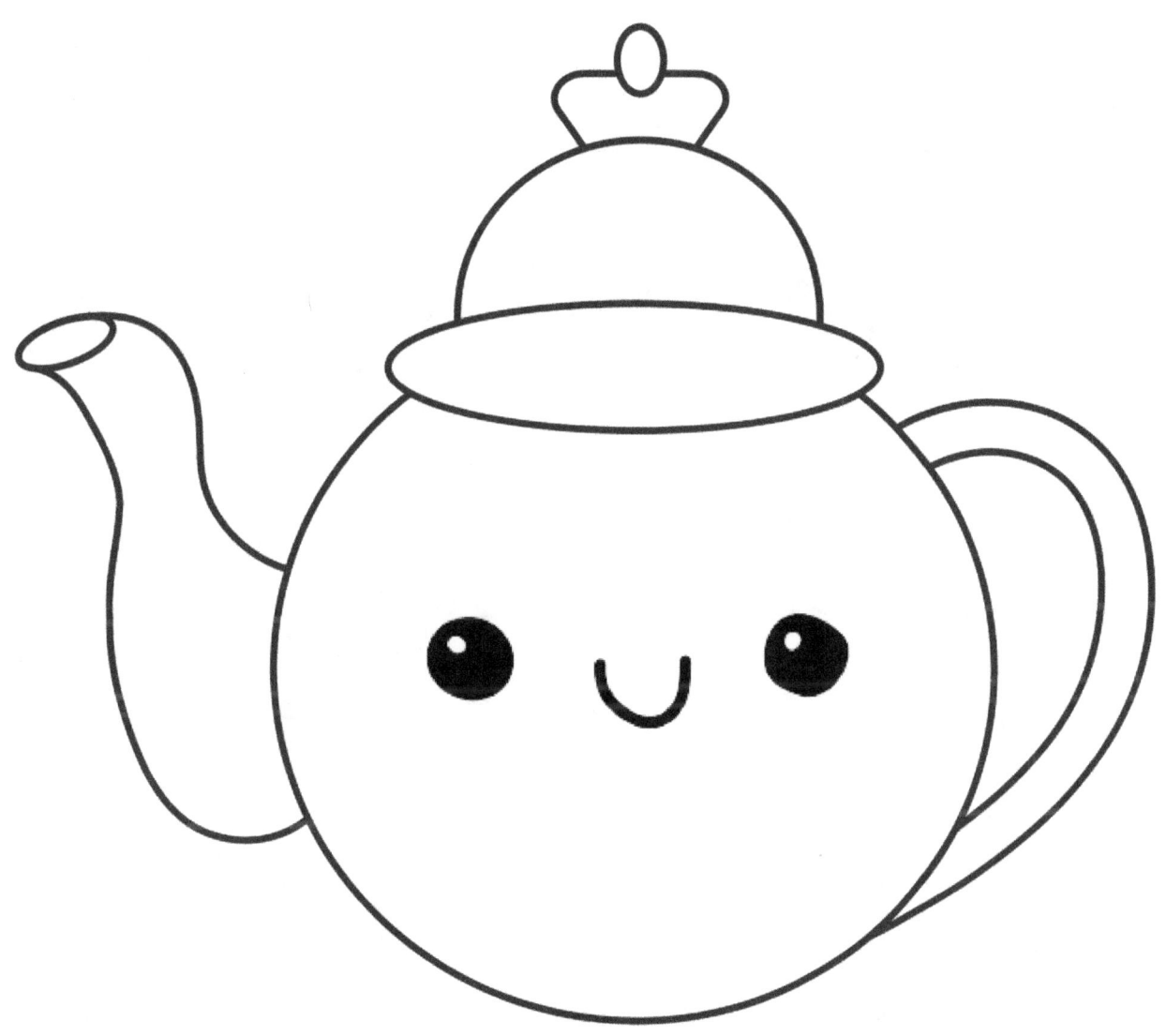

MILKSHAKE

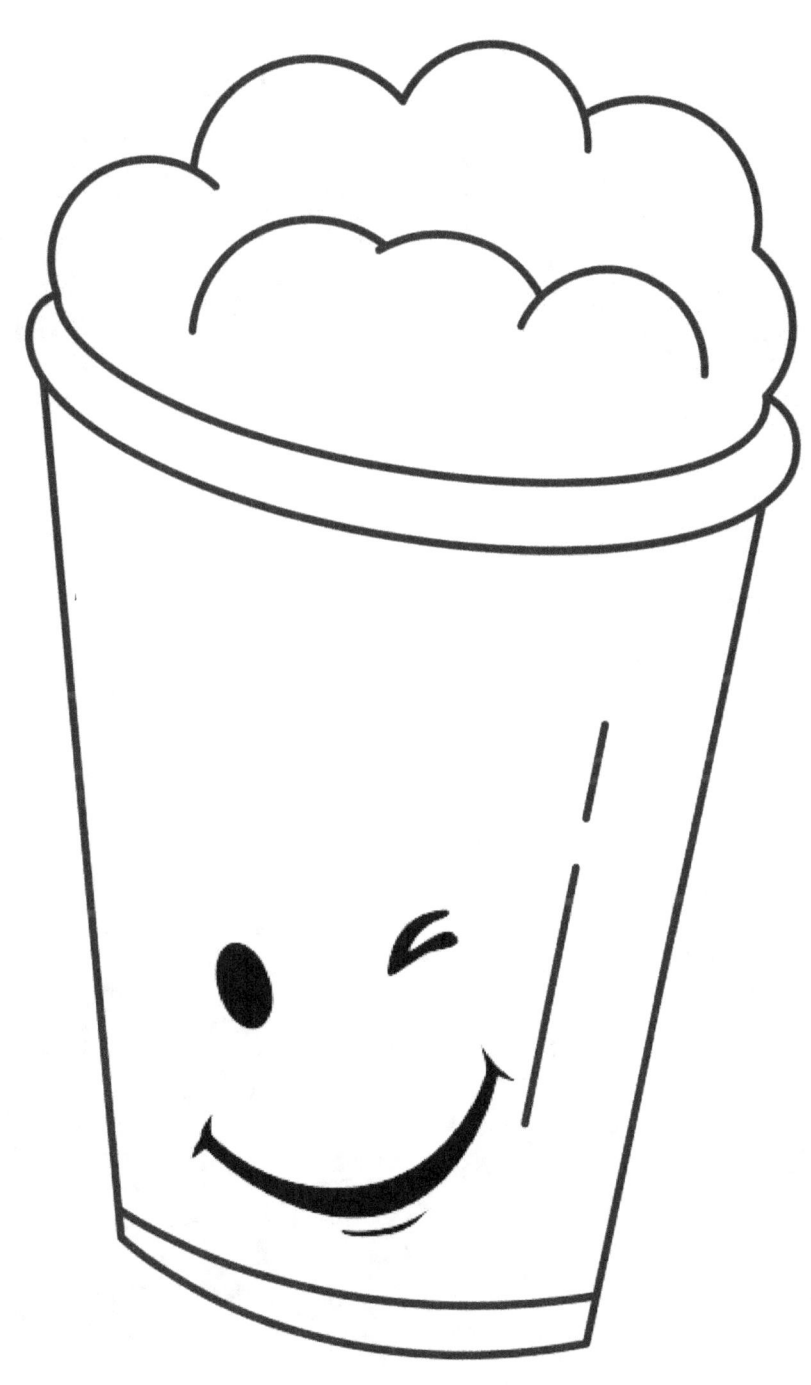

SANDWICHE

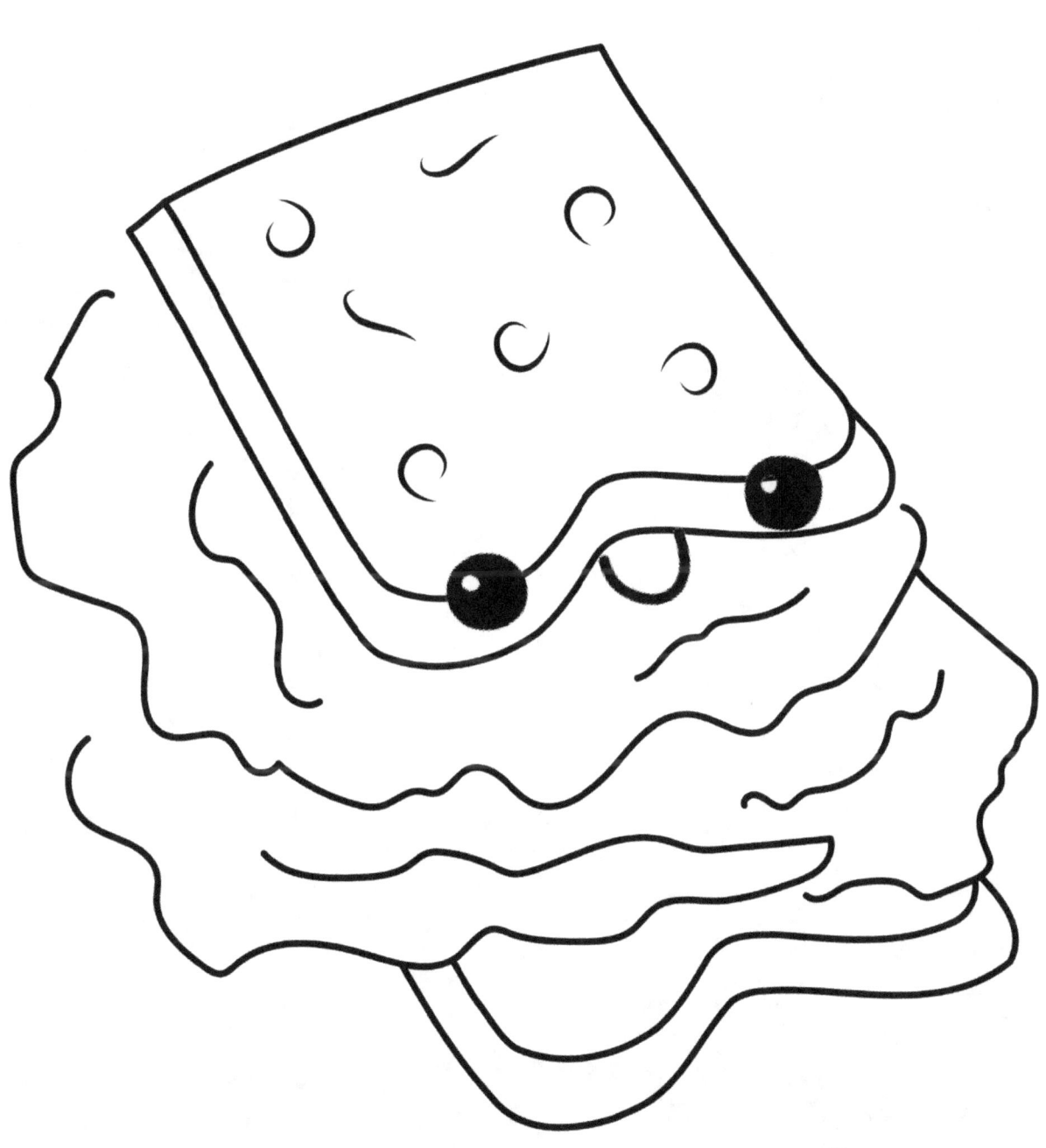

BURRITO

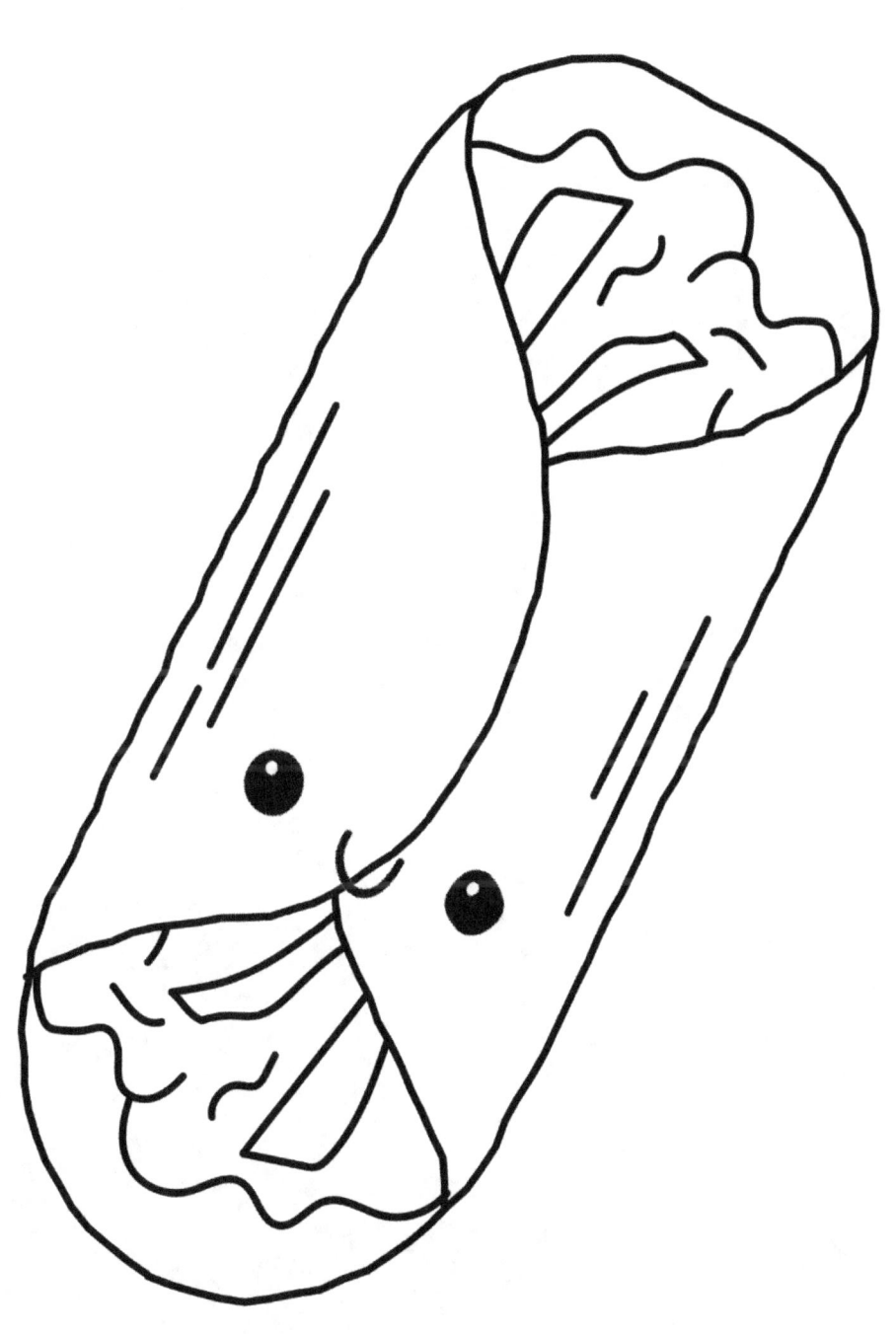

ICE CREAM

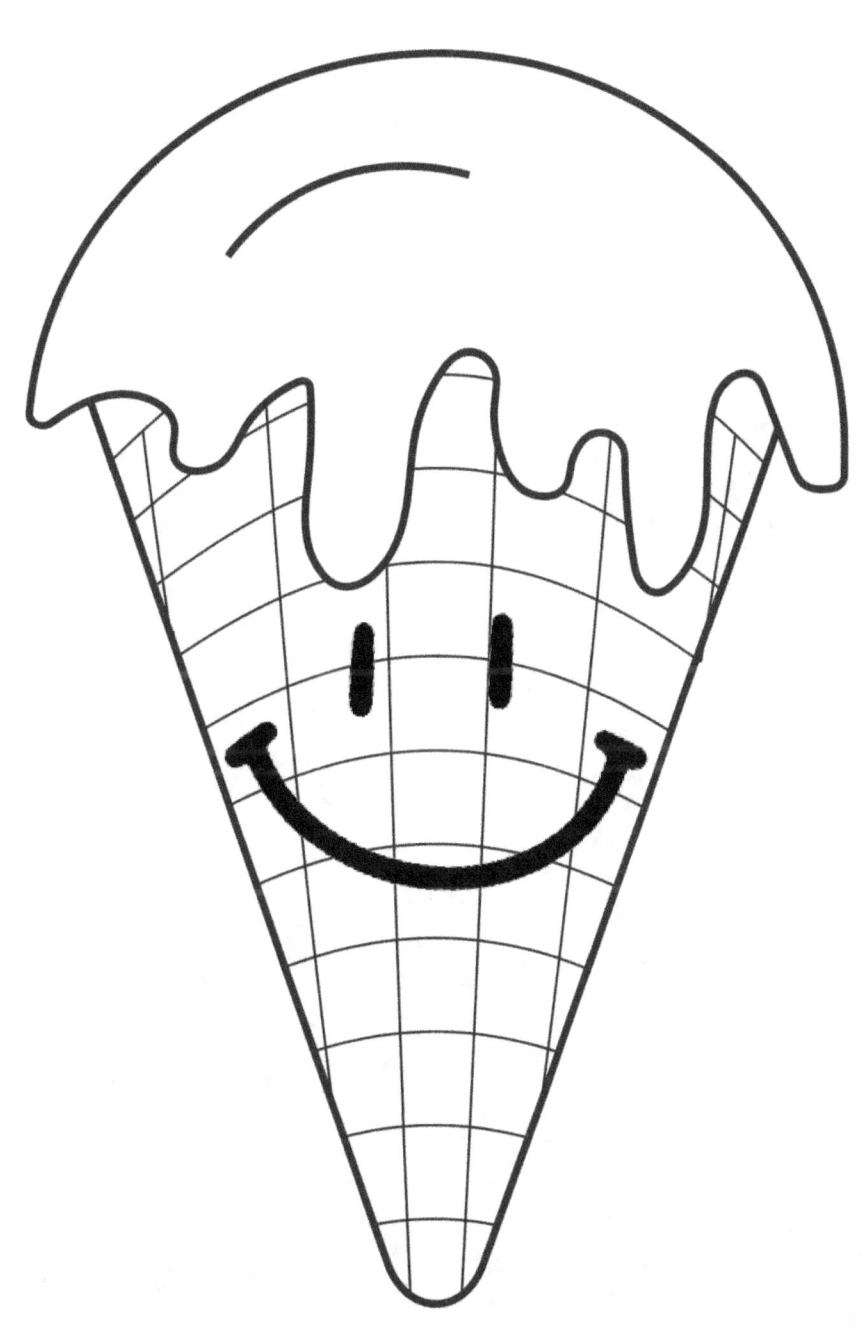

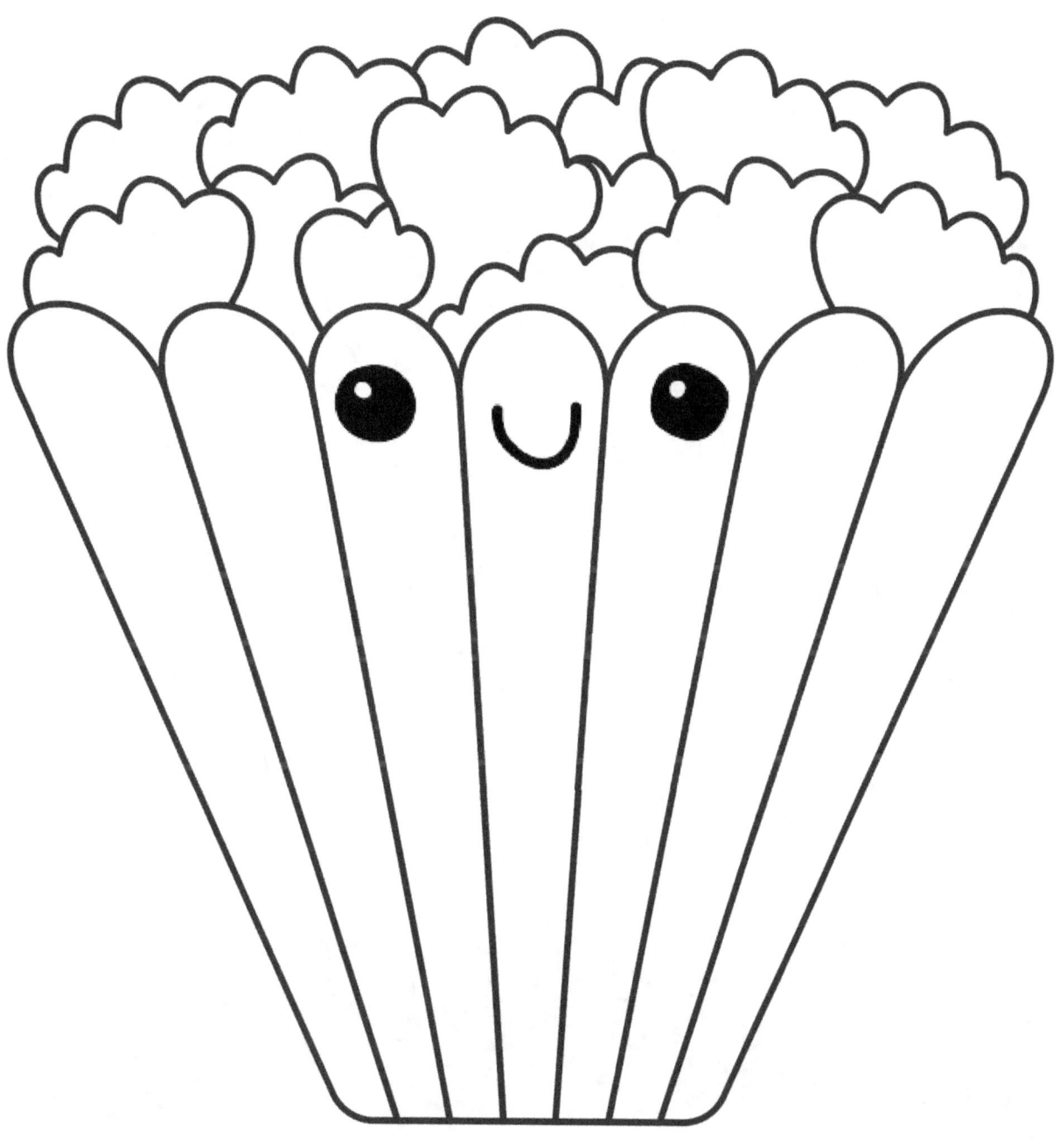

DONUT

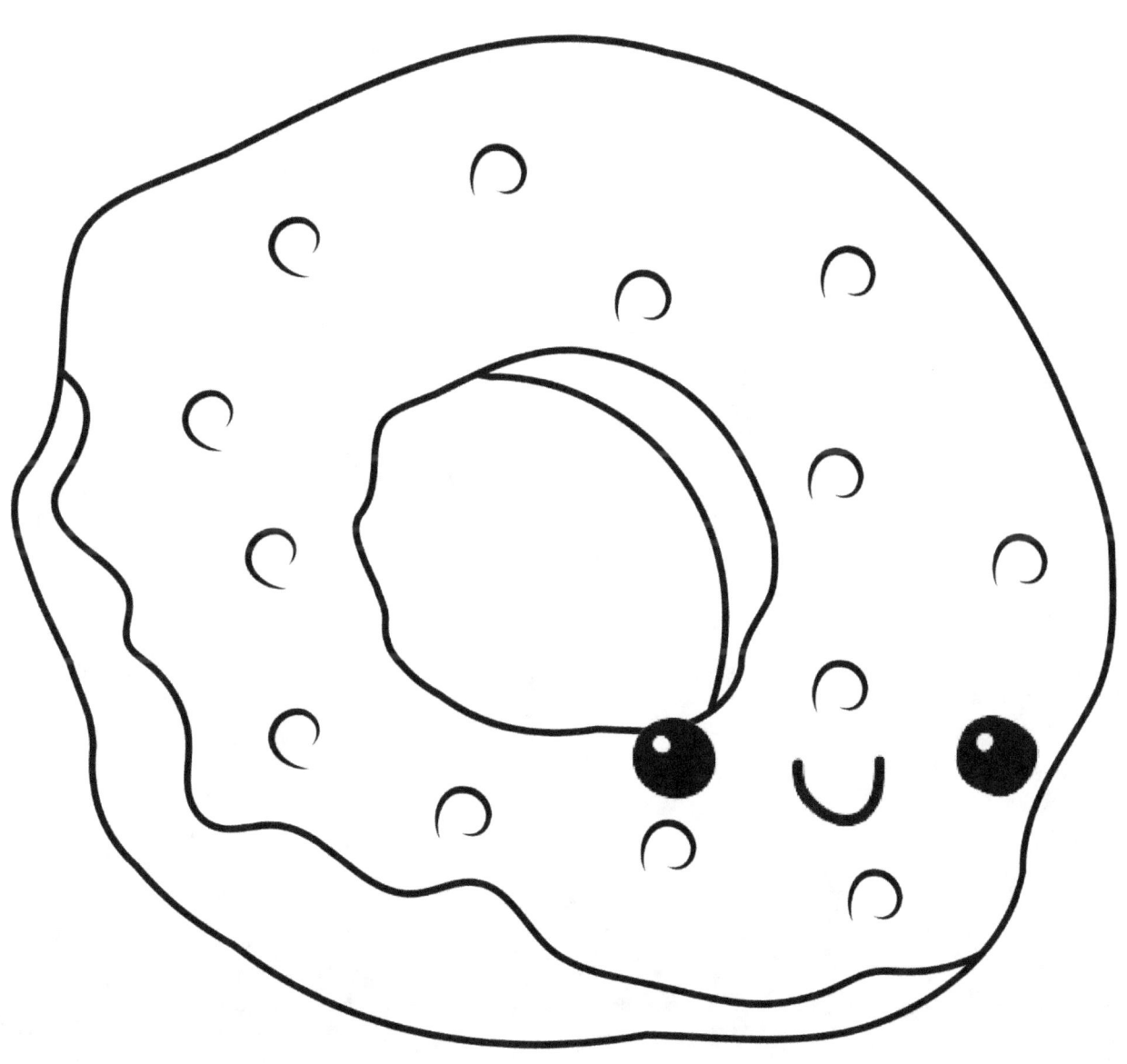

CANTALOUPE

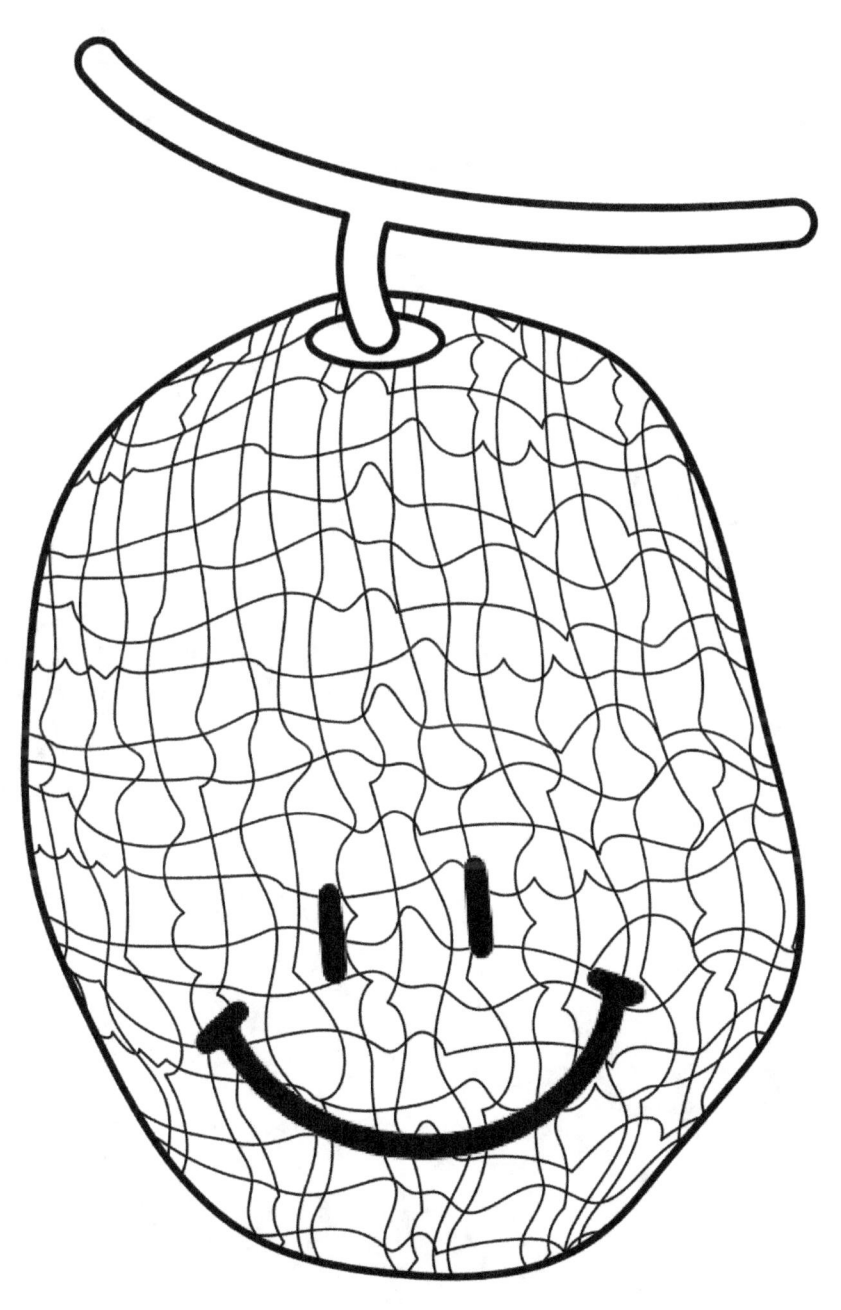

TACOS

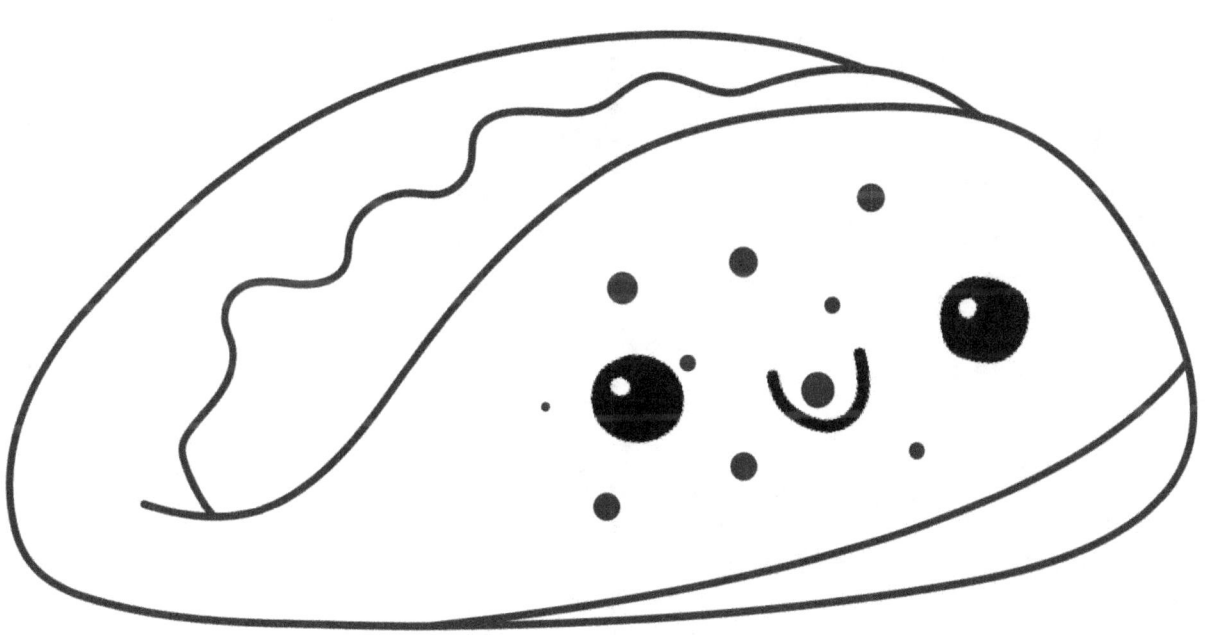

BURGER

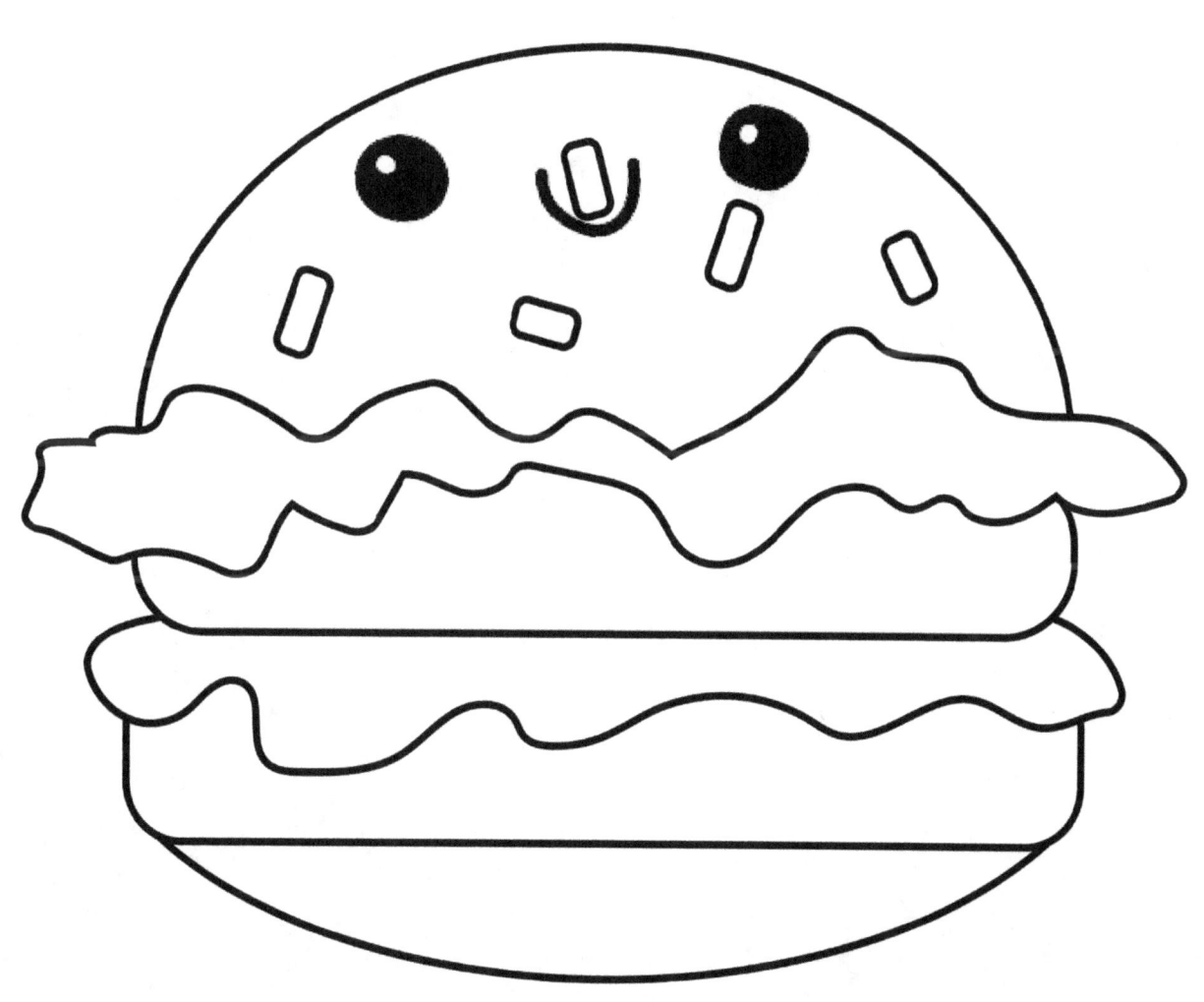

CRACKER

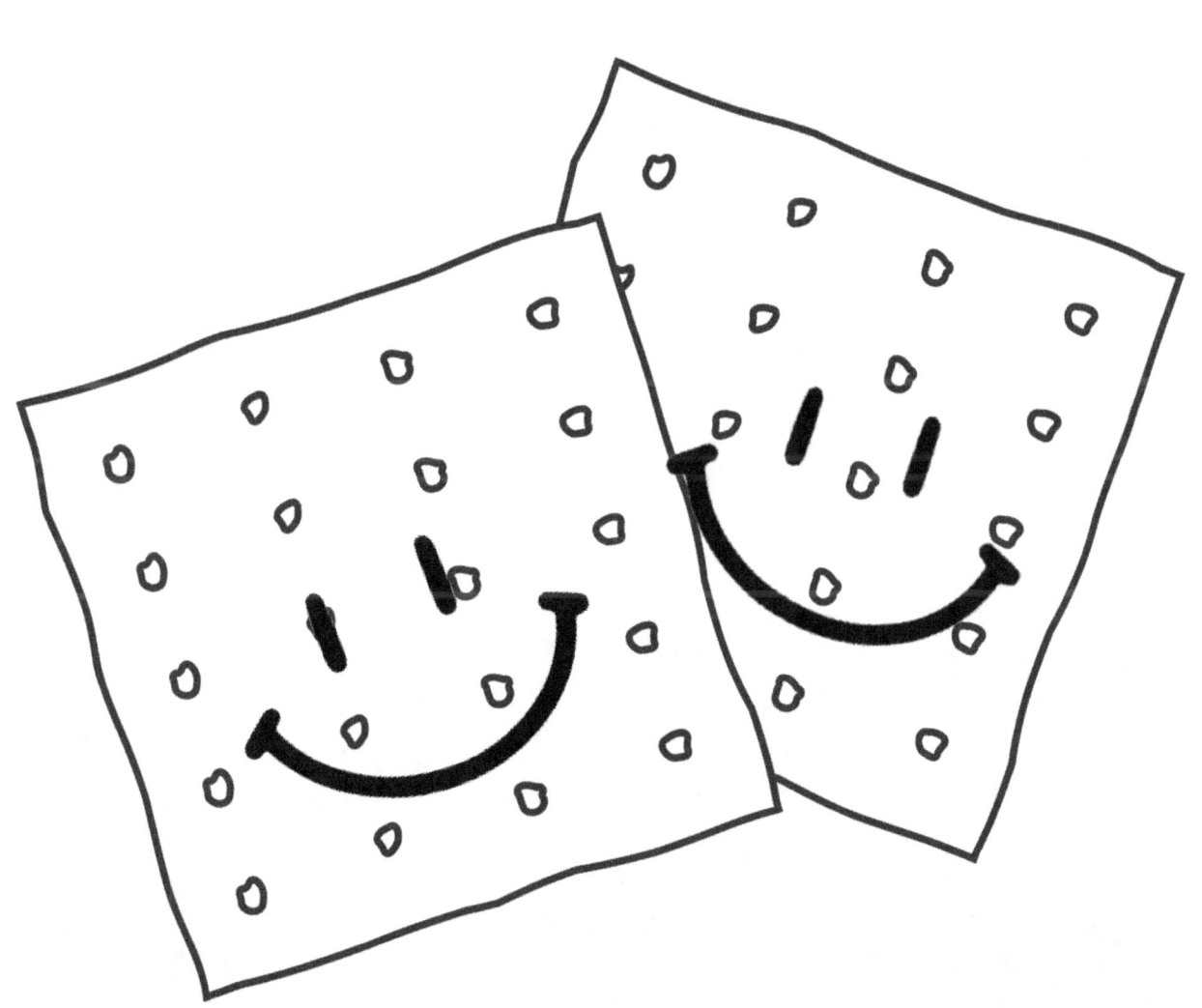

PIZZA SLICE

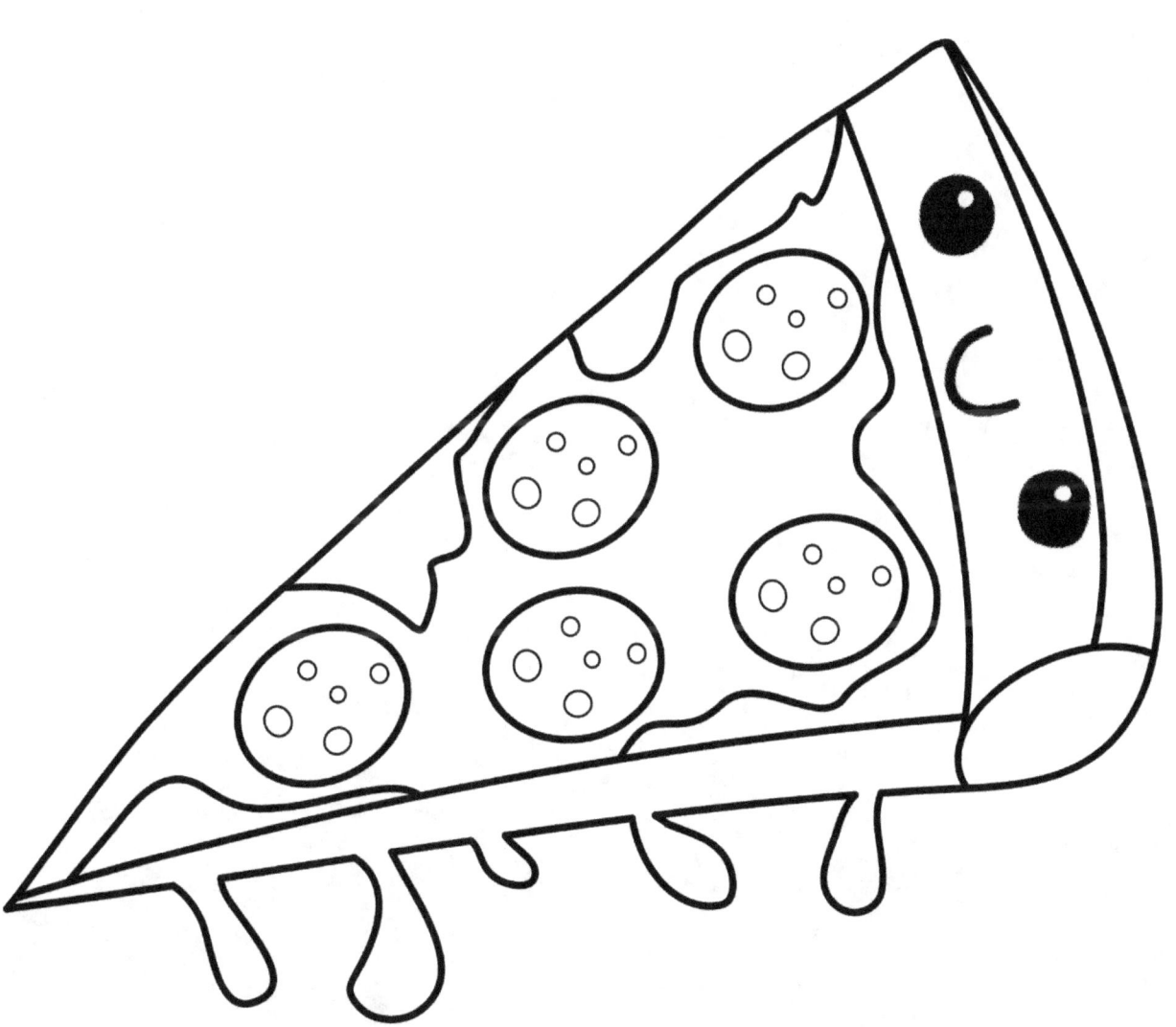

PINEAPPLE

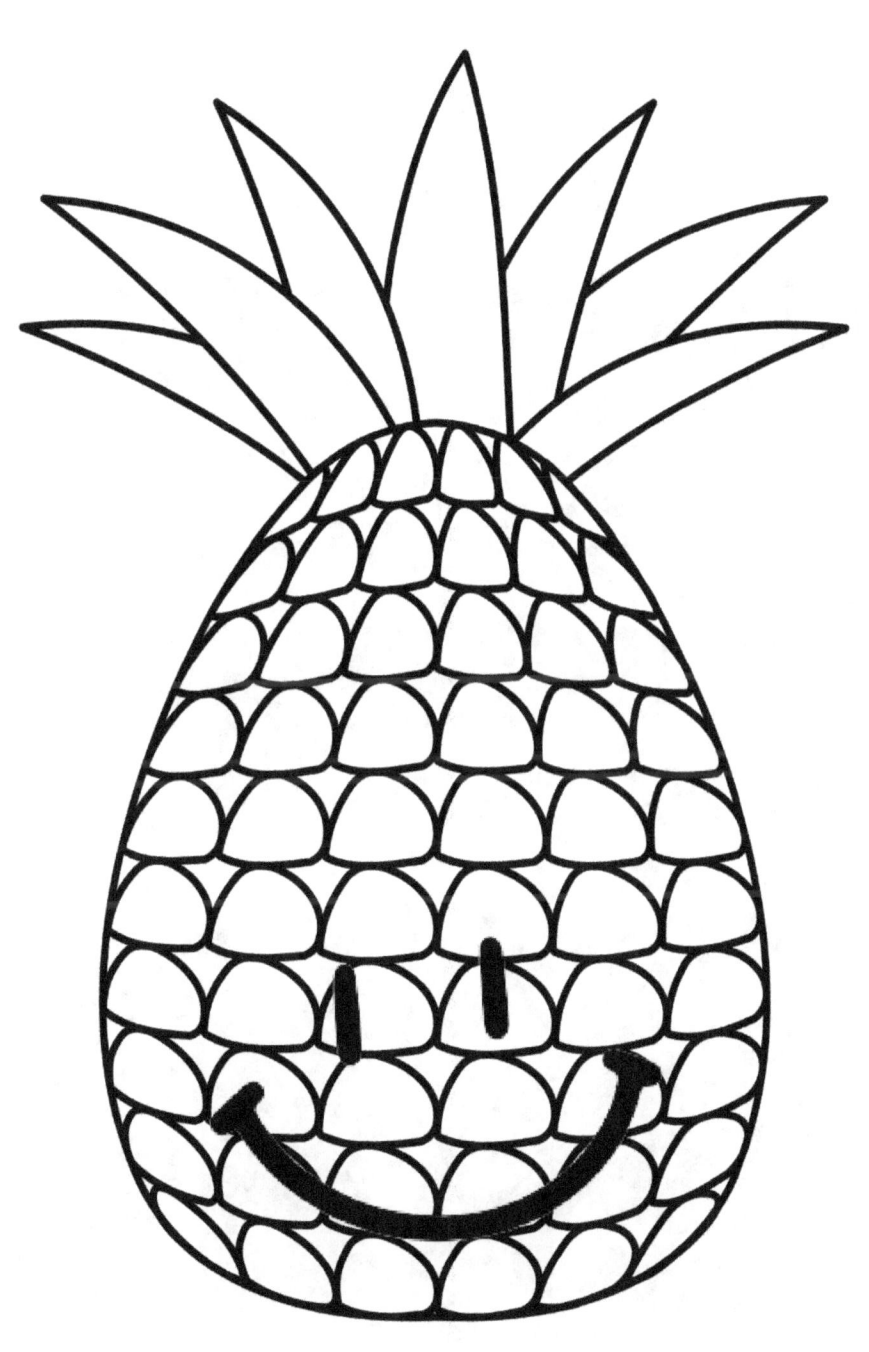

PANCAKE

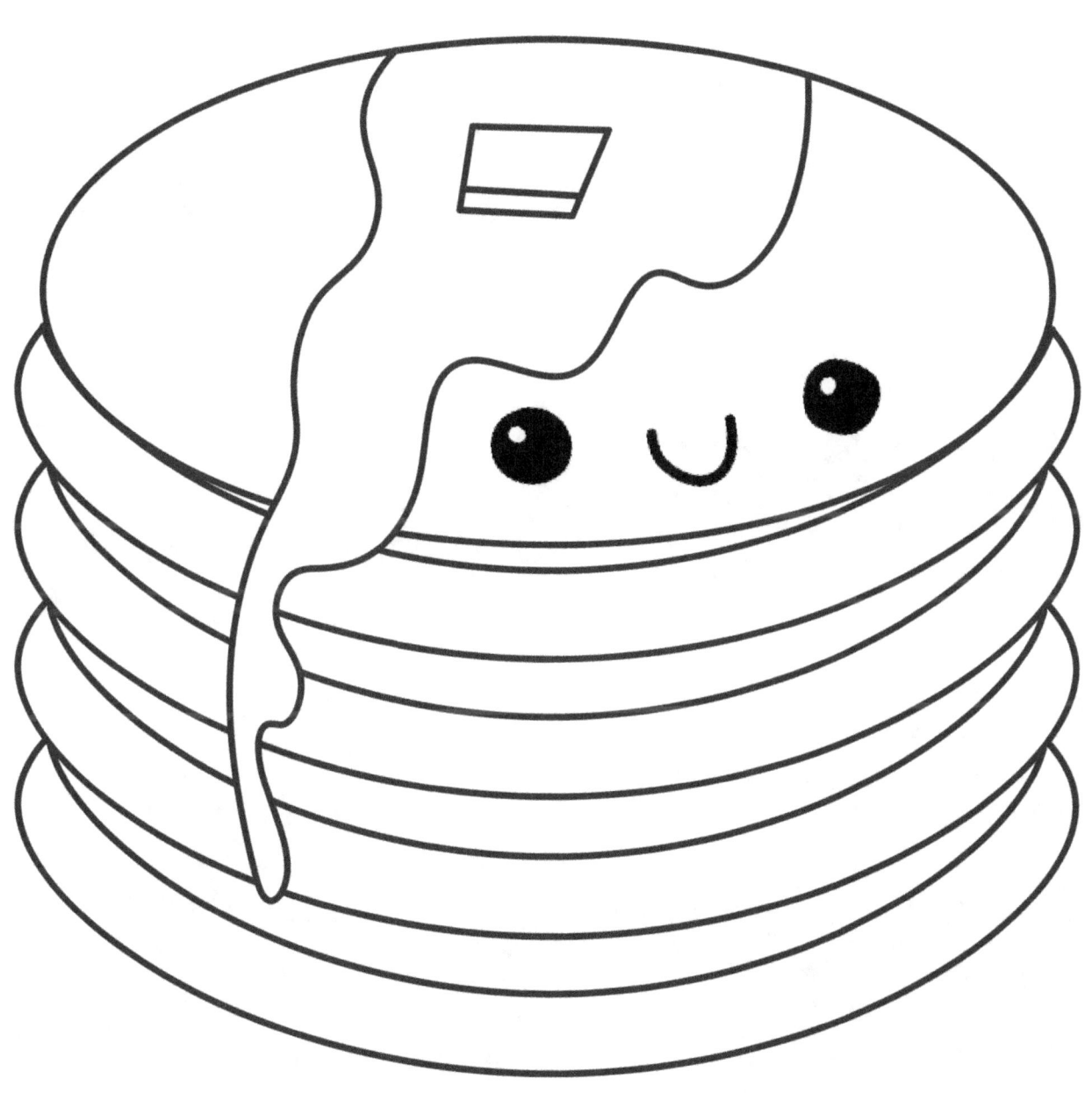

POTATO CHIPS

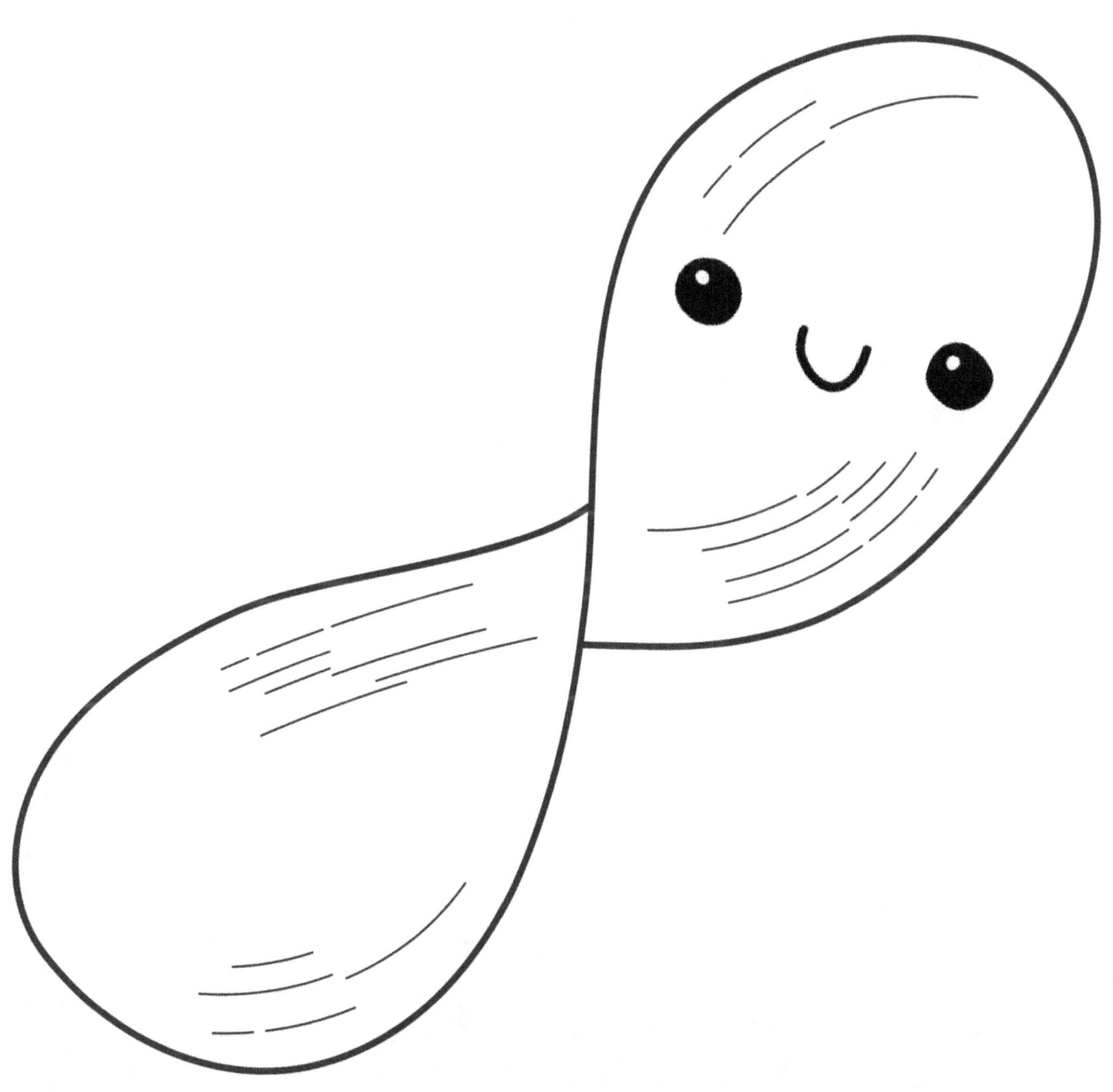

CAKE

www.ingramcontent.com/pod-product-compliance
Lightning Source LLC
Chambersburg PA
CBHW082357220526
45470CB00008B/2780